Key Concepts in
Educational Assessment

Recent volumes include:

Key Concepts in Tourism and Research
David Botterill and Vincent Platenkamp

Key Concepts in Sport and Exercise Research Methods
Michael Atkinson

Key Concepts in Media and Communications
Paul Jones and David Holmes

Key Concepts in Sport Psychology
John M. D. Kremer, Aidan Moran, Graham Walker and Cathy Craig

Fifty Key Concepts in Gender Studies
Jane Pilcher and Imelda Whelehan

Key Concepts in Medical Sociology
Jonathan Gabe, Mike Bury and Mary Ann Elston

Key Concepts in Leisure Studies
David Harris

Key Concepts in Urban Studies
Mark Gottdiener and Leslie Budd

The SAGE Key Concepts series provides students with accessible and authoritative knowledge of the essential topics in a variety of disciplines. Cross-referenced throughout, the format encourages critical evaluation through understanding. Written by experienced and respected academics, the books are indispensable study aids and guides to comprehension.

TINA ISAACS, CATHERINE ZARA
AND GRAHAM HERBERT WITH
STEVEN J. COOMBS AND CHARLES SMITH

Key Concepts in
Educational Assessment

Los Angeles | London | New Delhi
Singapore | Washington DC

Los Angeles | London | New Delhi
Singapore | Washington DC

SAGE Publications Ltd
1 Oliver's Yard
55 City Road
London EC1Y 1SP

SAGE Publications Inc.
2455 Teller Road
Thousand Oaks, California 91320

SAGE Publications India Pvt Ltd
B 1/I 1 Mohan Cooperative Industrial Area
Mathura Road
New Delhi 110 044

SAGE Publications Asia-Pacific Pte Ltd
3 Church Street
#10-04 Samsung Hub
Singapore 049483

Editor: Jude Bowen
Assistant editor: Miriam Davey
Project manager: Jeanette Graham
Production editor: Nicola Marshall
Copyeditor: Sharon Cawood
Proofreader: Beth Crockett
Marketing manager: Lorna Patkai
Cover design: Wendy Scott
Typeset by: C&M Digitals (p) Ltd, Chennai, India
Printed and bound by CPI Group (UK) Ltd,
Croydon, CR0 4YY

Library of Congress Control Number: 2012944435

British Library Cataloguing in Publication data

A catalogue record for this book is available from
the British Library

MIX
Paper from
responsible sources
FSC
www.fsc.org   FSC® C013604

ISBN 978-1-4462-1056-7
ISBN 978-1-4462-1057-4 (pbk)

contents

contents

key concepts in educational assessment

about the authors

Tina Isaacs is a Senior Lecturer at the Institute of Education, University of London and is Programme Leader for the MA in Educational Assessment. Prior to joining the Institute, she spent 15 years working for the National Council for Vocational Qualifications (NCVQ), the Qualifications and Curriculum Authority (QCA) and the Office of Qualifications and Examinations Regulation (Ofqual), where she was the Head of 14–19 Regulation.

Catherine Zara has a wide range of experience in the fields of lifelong learning and workforce development, and in the assessment and evaluation of vocational, professional and occupational learning. Most recently she was Director of the MA in Educational Assessment and Director of the BA (Hons) in Post Compulsory Education and Training at the University of Warwick.

Graham Herbert became the Deputy Head of the CIEA prior to its launch in 2006. He has been responsible for a large portfolio of programmes, in particular the development of the Chartered Educational Assessor (CEA) programme, developing the postgraduate diploma in educational assessment and supporting the development of Masters degrees. Prior to that, he was a teacher and senior examiner for both general and vocational examinations.

Steven J. Coombs has been the Head of the CPD department at Bath Spa University (BSU) since 2002. From August 2000 until August 2002, Steve worked as Professor of Educational Technology at Sonoma State University, California, where he was involved in developing an educational technology research project as part of a large US initiative. Prior to that Steve was appointed for three years as Professor of Instructional Technology at the National Institute of Education in Singapore.

Charles Smith is senior lecturer in economics and education at Swansea Metropolitan, University of Wales Trinity St David. He has taught in the secondary, further education and university sectors, and has served as a primary school governor. As a senior examiner and consultant with several awarding bodies, he has been involved in all major reforms in the UK assessment system since the mid-1980s, and has led staff development in learning, teaching and assessment in a wide range of countries.

preface

Because assessment is now central to much of what we do, educationalists are regularly exposed to key assessment terms. So terms such as valid, reliable, assessment for learning and assessment of learning (sometimes referred to as formative assessment and summative assessment respectively) and feedback are widely used – yet not always defined. This may lead to confusion when we talk as if we mean the same thing while having different interpretations of the terms. *Key Concepts in Educational Assessment* is therefore a valuable and timely resource that provides clear definitions and explanations of significant assessment terms. In doing this it offers a wealth of examples from familiar assessment contexts to illustrate these meanings. This will be welcomed by students, teachers and lecturers at a time when, given the ever-widening role of assessment and the many changes in what is assessed, 'assessment literacy' has never been more important. I congratulate the authors in recognising the need for such a publication and for producing such an accessible and useful glossary.

Gordon Stobart
Emeritus Professor of Education
Institute of Education, University of London

key concepts in educational assessment

Introduction

Educational assessment is a well-established and deep, if not even, field of research and practice. It engages those enchanted by the intellectual and technical skills required for finely calibrated item definition, valid and reliable test design, or analysis of statistical data generated by ranges of scores. It intrigues newly qualified educationalists passionate about learning for its own sake and charged with the responsibility of enabling learners to demonstrate levels of attainment. It animates and frustrates professional teachers and lecturers who have demonstrated a lifelong commitment to helping their students become the best that they can be. And it is surprisingly absent as a well-developed discourse in many teacher training programmes at all levels of educational provision, in many countries. However, we fully recognise the importance of *assessment* – the planned and systematic process of gathering and interpreting evidence about learning in order to make a judgement about that learning – to the educational and economic policy of any country, and the contested nature of the relationship between formal educational assessment systems adopted and pedagogical approaches implemented in educational establishments.

The idea of a text on *Key Concepts in Educational Assessment* originated in a discussion with teacher training students about the lack of a good reference in which contemporary terminology, definitions and contested debates were located in one place, as a starting point for further enquiry. This discussion took place at a time when the authors were working with the Chartered Institute of Educational Assessors (CIEA) and colleagues from other UK universities to develop a suite of postgraduate programmes in educational assessment as a specialist subject for experienced educational professionals. It quickly became obvious to those colleagues and the CIEA that not only would our own particular students and members benefit from such a text but that it could benefit teachers, trainers, lecturers and assessors at all levels of educational provision. All of the authors are currently based in the UK, though not all are of British origin, and between us we have experience of educational provision in the USA, Malaysia, Singapore, Hong Kong, China, the Republic of Ireland, South Africa, Finland, Norway, France, Spain and the Middle East. The text is therefore located primarily in a UK context. However, it is also informed by our various international perspectives and experiences but does not purport to represent these evenly or comprehensively.

Deciding what to include in this first edition of the book has been tricky. There were obvious contenders, such as Validity, Reliability, Assessment of Learning (Summative) and Assessment for Learning (Formative). In relation to our choice of the rest, we must thank reviewers, expert and lay readers for insisting we add or drop certain items, but the final responsibility for what has been included here is ours. The entries are of various lengths, which reflect what we believe to be their relative importance and/or complexity. We supplement entries with suggestions for further reading about the concepts. However, we recognise that educational assessment is not a fixed entity and as new systems and concepts are developed and evolve, it is our intention to update and provide future revisions of this book.

The original students who suggested the book, and several others too, have been kind enough to read and comment on its contents and have thereby helped to make it what we hope is an invaluable starting point and regular point of reference for those working and/or studying in this intriguing field. Any errors or infelicities are, of course, ours. We hope that this book both informs and illuminates the reader to the links between pedagogy and assessment.

HOW TO USE THIS BOOK

The key concepts are listed alphabetically and each begins with a very short definition. The entries provide some background information on the topic, generally followed by a more analytical discussion that highlights changes to the topic over time, issues, debates and controversies. None of the concepts is straightforward and while we have tried to present things in a way that most viewpoints are aired, this doubtless has not always been possible to every reader's satisfaction.

Many of the concepts are interrelated, but we have no expectations that anyone will read the book from cover to cover, so we have sometimes repeated information in more than one entry. Where there is a direct link between concepts, we have referred to other concepts within the entry and highlighted those relationships in bold so that you can easily find and read through related entries.

Each entry has suggestions for further reading. Some of these suggestions are seminal works in the field; others are of a more recent vintage. We hope that these will get you started if you are seeking out additional information. Each entry is fully referenced and all of the references are in the back of the book, including website addresses where relevant. We have dispensed with the often used 'last accessed' element of the addresses because we do not believe that it adds very much pertinent information. At the time of writing, all of the addresses were live. Information in printed texts in this fast-moving field gets out of date quickly, though, especially in the more policy-related entries, something of which we are acutely aware. What was a government strategy in 2012 may not still be in place in 2013, much to the chagrin of educators who have to cope with policy and guidance overload.

Finally, while we tried to cover the essential concepts in the field of educational assessment, we doubtless have failed to explore all of them, or explore them to everyone's satisfaction. We therefore hope that you see this book as the start of further and deeper discussion about educational assessment and as a beginning point from which you can branch out and find your own definitions and interpretations.

introduction

Accreditation of Prior Learning (APL)

APL recognises learning that has taken place due to prior study, work or life experience, and allows colleges and universities to give credit for these, allowing students to follow a process in order to obtain credit for a module or unit that forms part of a course or qualification, instead of formally studying or gathering new evidence. For credibility, APL requires an assessment process, which replicates and gives equivalence to the assessment of a taught module or assessed unit of competence.

TERMINOLOGY

APL and APEL (Accreditation of Prior Experiential Learning) are often used interchangeably, but they are not synonymous. The Quality and Assurance Agency (QAA) uses the term APCL (Accreditation for Previous Certificated Learning) to refer to prior learning that has been accredited and where a formal record, such as a certificate, has been issued. APEL refers to learning that arises out of reflection on previous work or life experience. APL is an umbrella term, covering both APEL and APCL.

QAA GUIDELINES

The QAA is the higher education regulator in the UK. It takes the view that APL is consistent with a number of broad objectives: lifelong learning; social inclusion; wider participation; employability; and partnerships with business and community organisations. APEL, in particular, opens up opportunities for social and ethnic groups, which are under-represented in higher education, and people who might be operating at high levels at work or in the community, but lack paper **qualifications**.

QUALITY ASSURANCE

A key issue is that previous experience or studies on their own do not guarantee APL. It is the relevant *learning* that has resulted from this previous experience or study that is crucial. To obtain APL for all or part of a qualification, programme or module of study, students must provide evidence, perhaps in portfolio form, or through interviews, artefacts or written reflections, that they have achieved knowledge and understanding equivalent to the learning outcomes for which they are seeking credit.

Students claiming APCL might find that a certain amount of double-counting is permitted. In other words, a certificate that contributed to a qualification already obtained might also be allowed to contribute towards another qualification. This could happen in the teaching profession, for example, where some modules for a basic teaching qualification, the Postgraduate Certificate in Education (PGCE), are passed at Level 7 and then some credits from those modules might later be accepted as APCL for a higher degree, such as a Masters degree (MA).

ACCEPTABILITY AND AUTHENTICITY

It is essential that APL should not be a mere formality. Complacent use of APL by educational institutions would undermine its credibility. Students should be put through a tailored process that generates evidence that can be verified and that is equivalent to written evidence from coursework or examinations. This evidence should be in a form that can be submitted to an external examiner and considered by an **awarding body**. In a higher education context, APL is best regarded as being a type of 'module' and will attract a fee in recognition of tutorial, administrative and assessment costs. The National Vocational Qualification (NVQ) system also recognises Prior Learning (PL), Accreditation of Prior Learning (APL), Accreditation of Prior Experiential Learning (APEL) and Accreditation of Prior Achievement (APA). These processes have been devised to enable achievement from a range of activities to be counted towards an award. In order to assess the extent to which they demonstrate this, evidence of such activities must be mapped against the requirements of a given unit, part-unit or qualification. Such evidence must be valid, authentic, current, relevant and sufficient.

FURTHER READING:

Evans, N. (2000). *Experiential Learning Around the World: Employability and the Global Economy.* London: Jessica Kingsley Publishers.

Quality Assurance Agency (2004). *Guidelines on the Accreditation of Prior Learning.* London: QAA.

Tummons, J. (2011). Assessing *Learning in the Lifelong Learning Sector.* Exeter: Learning Matters.

Assessment for Learning

Assessment for learning is the process of seeking and interpreting evidence for use by learners and their teachers to decide where the learners are in their learning, where they need to go and how best to get there (Assessment Reform Group, 2002: 1).

Assessment for Learning (AfL) was a term made popular in the UK by Black and Wiliam (1998a, 1998b) when locating teacher and student feedback as part of the assessment and learning process. AfL promoted the sharing of criteria with learners, the effective use of classroom 'talk' and questioning, and supported peer and self-assessment as part of the assessment and learning process (Swaffield, 2009). It represented a challenge to the ascendency of summative assessment and a turn (or return) towards the personalisation of learning, in schools in particular. It was further linked to conceptualising curriculum assessment activities (Black *et al.*, 2003) as part of an ongoing formative assessment process.

However, AfL as a formative assessment strategy (Clarke, 2005) goes back arguably as far as John Dewey's (Dewey *et al.*, 1987, 1988) seminal works linking active learning with meaningful experience and motivation.

key concepts in educational assessment

6

Indeed, a pedagogical strategy that encourages action learning tasks and assessment strategies is something also suggested by von Cranach and Harré (1982) in their goal-directed activity theory. This concept was further refined by critical theorists such as David Boud (1988) who suggested the benefits and practice of student-centred and autonomous learning that underpins much of the pedagogical aspirations of AfL. Dylan Wiliam (2011) traces the history of AfL from the early 20th century, stressing the importance of individualising instruction, assessment and **feedback** to suit the variety of student needs.

From these ideas, the concept of feedback as an important stage within the human learning process developed, something that Black and Wiliam (1998b) suggested was of vital importance to classroom-based learning. A later publication by Black *et al.* (2003), *Assessment for Learning: Putting it into Practice*, provided a pedagogical rationale that combines the notion of feedback with **self-assessment** and formative assessment:

> an assessment activity can help learning if it provides information to be used as feedback by teachers and their students in assessing themselves and each other, to modify the teaching and learning activities in which they are engaged. Such assessment becomes formative assessment when the evidence is used to adapt the teaching work to meet the learning needs. (Black *et al.*, 2003: 2)

More recently, a group of scholars meeting in Dunedin, New Zealand in 2009 agreed the following definition: 'assessment for learning is part of everyday practice by students, teachers and peers that seeks, reflects upon and responds to information from dialogue, demonstration and observation in ways that enhance ongoing learning' (cited in Crooks, 2011: 71–2).

Citing Brookhart, Wiliam (2011) charts the evolution of formative assessment, which he characterises as nested:

- Formative assessment provides information about the learning process
- Formative assessment provides information about the learning process that teachers can use for instructional decisions
- Formative assessment provides information about the learning process that teachers can use for instructional decisions and students can use in improving their performance
- Formative assessment provides information about the learning process that teachers can use for instructional decisions and students can use in improving their performance, which motivates students (p. 8).

The Assessment Reform Group, which originally commissioned Black and Wiliam's work, defined AfL as 'the process of seeking and interpreting evidence for use by learners and their teachers to decide where the learners are in their learning, where they need to go and how best to get there' (2002: 1). They developed 10 key AfL principles that state that Assessment for Learning:

1 is part of effective planning
2 focuses on how pupils learn
3 is central to classroom practice
4 is a key professional skill
5 is sensitive and constructive
6 fosters motivation
7 promotes understanding of goals and criteria
8 helps learners know how to improve
9 develops the capacity for self [and peer] assessment
10 recognises all educational achievement.

Implementation of the three factors identified by the Assessment Reform Group can take place in a variety of ways: The first, judgements about where learners are in their learning, can be made through diagnostic assessment such as listening to children read and gleaning information from class work or tests. Open-ended 'rich' questions can involve students more deeply, engage them collaboratively in problem-solving techniques and provide opportunities for teachers to ascertain any misconceptions students might have.

The second, moving students forward to what they need to learn, involves a clear statement of learning criteria, building on current learning and explaining why the learning is important. Finally, the best way to achieve this is through feedback and feed forward, most useful when effectively timed and clearly linked to the learning intention. It needs to be part of the understood success criteria, focus on task rather than ego, give clues on how to bridge gaps, offer strategies rather than solutions, challenge, require action and be achievable (Stobart, 2011).

Black and Wiliam (1998a) describe what goes on in classrooms where assessment aids learning. Typically, classroom practices include: observing students and listening to them describe what they are doing and the reasoning behind their actions; using open-ended questioning, which gets students to articulate their ideas; setting tasks that require students to apply skills and ideas; encouraging students to communicate their learning through actions as well as writing; and discussion rather than dialogue.

Further work on AfL, such as that by Mary James and her colleagues (2007), focused on making learning explicit, emphasising learner autonomy and shifting the focus from performance to actual learning (Swaffield, 2009). This means constantly checking the effects of certain practices and turning away from procedure-based activity.

Regarding the validity of assessment for learning, Crooks cites the following variables as being crucial:

- the relevance of the assessment evidence to the intended learning outcomes
- the degree to which the achievement of each learning outcome has been sampled
- how well the evidence focuses on performance at the intended time, or (where progress is the focus) on progress over the intended time period
- the fairness to all students of the processes and judgement during assessment
- the extent to which the evidence coalesces into coherent and meaningful pictures of performance (Crooks, 2011: 72).

Crooks (2011) highlights six key factors in effective assessment for learning: (1) committed, motivated participants – both teachers and students; (2) students' trust, so that they can be comfortable in admitting they need help; (3) students' understanding of the goals to which they are working; (4) learning goals of an appropriate level of challenge; (5) development of students' self-assessment skills; and (6) insight on the part of the person giving feedback (teachers or peers) into the difficulties a student might be having, providing feedback when students are most receptive and excellent judgement in framing comments appropriately, and tailoring them to each individual's needs.

The OECD considers AfL as an important part of a general international education policy to push formative assessment in secondary schools. The OECD (2005) published its findings in a policy brief article highlighting the benefits of formative assessment, in particular, achievement gains and equity of student outcomes. It emphasised that formative assessment builds students' learning to learn skills through: 'involving students as partners in that process' (OECD, 2005: 2). The OECD also identifies the tension between summative and formative assessment approaches and advises national policy makers to avoid 'high visibility summative assessments' as they are a 'significant barrier to formative practice' (OECD, 2005: 6). The challenge is in getting the balance right between summative and formative assessment systems.

Hutchinson and Young (2011) analyse the role of assessment for learning in Scotland, where the government has supported this type of assessment for a decade through its Assessment is For Learning (AiFL) programme. That programme has not been an unmitigated success, partially because Scotland has combined assessment for learning with assessment for accountability. Hutchinson and Young point to the following problems: 'deeply ingrained beliefs about learning and assessment; different understandings of the language and terminology of assessment; lack of mutual professional trust; and reluctance to change practice and take professional risks and responsibility for judgments about learning' (p. 64). They suggest that only through shared understanding of what is important for students to learn, a framework of assessment arrangements, development of professional practice in assessment, adequate feedback to stakeholders and partners, and support from external agencies can assessment for learning truly thrive.

AfL has not been without misinterpretation or critical appraisal. The UK government adopted an Assessment for Learning Strategy (DCSF, 2008) that has been accused of bowdlerising the ARG's 10 principles to promote close focus on only two subjects, English and mathematics, and the frequent in-class 'formative' assessment of levels of attainment students achieved in each (Swaffield, 2009). With its tick-box approach, emphasis on data collection and direct relationship to summative national curriculum assessment, the Strategy's misappropriation of the term AfL undermined formative assessment in schools in England. Coombs and McKenna (2009) also reported that AfL in English schools suffered a patchy implementation due to a lack of any national coordinated and embedded continuing professional development (CPD).

AfL's critics get scant attention, since the concept is almost universally acclaimed. Smith and Gorard (2005) found that the progress of students in year 7 mixed-ability classrooms was less good for those who received formative feedback alone as opposed to those who received marks, grades and minimal comments. While acknowledging that some general practice associated with AfL can be helpful in the learning process, Bennett (2011) argues that with such a wide variety of practices, processes and methods routinely associated with AfL, no overall judgements about its effectiveness can legitimately be made. He questions claims that have been made about the effect size of assessment for learning interventions (between .4 and .7 in Black and Wiliam's famous 1998 analysis [Black and Wiliam, 1998a]) because the studies under consideration were too disparate to be summarised in a meaningful sense. He also believes that certain considerations such as domain specific needs, the amount of support that teachers need to utilise formative assessment effectively and the wider impact on the educational system have not been analysed sufficiently. There are also problems with under-researched issues associated with **measurement** principles, since assessment for learning relies on human judgement and inferences that can be made about student performance, which can lead to measurement error and bias. If the inferences are wrong, the basis for altering instruction could also be wrong; if the inferences are correct, but the changes to instruction are inappropriate, then learning will not be improved. Without a well-defined set of practices, Bennett posits that there will be a wide variety of outcomes from AfL.

In a special issue on formative assessment in Applied Measurement, Robert Shavelson (2008) stated:

> After five years of work, our euphoria devolved into a reality that formative assessment, like so many other education reforms, has a long way to go before it can be wielded masterfully by a majority of teachers to positive ends. This is not to discourage the formative assessment practice and research agenda. We do provide evidence that when used as intended, formative assessment might very well be a productive instructional tool. Rather, the special issue is intended to be a sobering call to the task ahead. (p. 294)

Many researchers, teachers and other stakeholders believe the challenge is worth taking up and continue to explore the efficacy of assessment for learning.

FURTHER READING

Assessment Reform Group (2002). *Assessment for Learning: 10 Principles. Research-based principles to guide classroom practice.* Available at: http://arrts.gtcni.org.uk/gtcni/bitstream/2428/4623/1/Assessment%20for%20Learning%20-%2010%20principles.pdf

Black, P. J., Harrison, C., Lee, C., Marshall, B. and Wiliam, D. (2003). *Assessment for Learning: Putting it into Practice.* Milton Keynes: Open University Press.

Wiliam, D. (2011). 'What is assessment for learning?'. *Studies in Educational Evaluation,* 37 (1), 3–14.

> Assessment of learning is also known as summative assess-
> ment, which is a success measure of the outcomes of the end of
> a unit, programme, year's study, qualification or educational
> experience (for example, school leaving examinations and cer-
> tificates). It is almost always a formal process and can include
> teacher judgement as well as testing.

It has been traditional in most countries for assessment to be closely associated in the minds of policy makers, parents, teachers and students with the
idea of summative assessment – the process of measuring students' learning at a set point in time against a set of standards. The most commonly
used summative assessment instruments are tests and examinations, but
this narrows the range of possibilities. Teacher judgements on evidence
such as homework, portfolios of achievement, the outcomes of formative
assessment, attendance, effort, etc. are routinely used summatively in countries such as the USA and Australia, and in the UK in Scotland through its
newly introduced Curriculum for Excellence. These judgements, however,
are generally used alongside testing, although in **vocational assessment**
teacher judgement can be the sole summative method.

Daniel Koretz (2008) in defining the most common form of summative assessment – tests – stresses that they can only measure a small
sub-set of what we ultimately want students to know and be able to do –
that is, of the goals of education. Tests can only sample students' knowledge, skills and understanding within any subject or sector and therefore
can only stand as proxies for 'better and more comprehensive measures
that we cannot obtain' (Koretz, 2008: 19).

Summative assessment leads to the award of **qualifications**: certificates, diplomas, degrees; and these are often awarded not just on a pass/
fail basis, but utilising a range of marks, **grades** and classifications.
Summative assessment can be used for a variety of purposes, among
them: to record achievement; to predict future achievement; to allow

key concepts in educational assessment

learners to progress to a higher level of study; to allow learners to enter into or progress within a workplace or a profession. It is, however, routinely used for other purposes, most notably in the USA and the UK, for school, regional and national monitoring and accountability (see below).

Since assessment of learning plays such a big role in students' futures, it is critical that testing systems are developed so that the inferences drawn from their outcomes are as **reliable** and **valid** as possible. Test scores can only reflect a small part of the behaviours we are trying to capture and are only of value if they can tell us something useful about the larger domain about which we seek information (Koretz, 2008). That means that the elements that comprise a test or examination – the items themselves, their *mark schemes* and their markers – need to be under constant scrutiny.

TEST DEVELOPMENT

Proper preparation of assessment instruments is crucial in assessment of learning. The assessment must carefully sample content and skills, ensuring that all the important elements in the learning programme are represented in a meaningful way. This means avoiding construct under-representation, where only some content is assessed – usually that which is easiest to test – and construct irrelevance, where extraneous content is assessed – such as reading skills in a mathematics test involving problem solving.

Starting from the learning outcomes, test developers construct a blueprint or test specification that spells out what should be tested and the weighting that each element should have. For example, although a test might include recall items those might be given a lesser weighting than items that require analysis or evaluation. Depending on what is being assessed, developers select the type of tasks – **select** and/or **supply** – and arrange them in a reasonable order. Generally, it is good to group items testing similar content or skills together and to begin with easier items, working up to the more difficult. This way the assessment will allow weaker candidates to grapple with manageable items at the outset. It is crucial that the directions for each item are clear and unambiguous. To **differentiate** appropriately among test takers, items need to be set at a level that will allow **discrimination,** that is, not too difficult or too easy. However, both easier and stretching and challenging items should also be included so that all test takers are confronted with items of appropriate challenge. If possible, assessments should be trialled or piloted before they are given to large groups of students.

Developing good **mark schemes** is as important as developing good test items, especially in large-scale testing, where there are many external markers. External markers must be properly trained, **standardised and moderated**. Outcomes can be reported back in terms of scores, marks, percentages, grades, levels or descriptions of achievement.

STANDARDS

Assessment of learning measures students' progress against standards, which represent the consistency of the level of demand in the education system. Standards can be expressed in a number of ways. Curriculum standards represent the depth and breadth of learning that students are required to demonstrate – what they are *expected* to know and are able to do, and what the course has set out to achieve. Examination or test standards can be found within what is being tested, that is, the items and tasks that students must carry out – what students can *show* they know and are able to do. Examination standards should be consistent with curriculum standards or the assessment instrument cannot be said to be reliable or valid. Performance standards refer to what students *actually achieve* – how well they have shown what they know and are able to do. A common metaphor that describes the relationship between curriculum and performance standards is that of a hurdle. Curriculum standards dictate how high the hurdle will be; performance standards concern how many people are able to jump over it.

Setting performance standards is one of the most difficult tasks in assessment, especially if the assessment instrument is being used for the first time and the assessment developers have few past instruments with which to compare it. **Comparability** of standards is more easily achieved in a mature assessment regime. Standards can be norm-based (or cohort-based) wherein a certain percentage of students will be said to achieve at each level, or criterion-based, where how well students achieve is based on how well they do against set attributes. However, it is important to note, as Angoff stated in 1974, that all **criterion-referenced** assessment is based on a set of normative assumptions (Wiliam, 2010b). The UK examination system is largely criterion-referenced and standards are set by a combination of human judgement and statistical evidence of students' prior performance, a system generally known as 'weak criterion-referencing' (Baird, 2007) because it includes other elements aside from whether or not students have fulfilled the assessment criteria.

ASSESSMENT OF LEARNING AND ACCOUNTABILITY

Assessment of learning, especially high-stakes examinations that are used for selection and progression purposes, receives a great deal of criticism. Sometimes this criticism is based on the assessment instruments themselves, for example teachers in England have questioned the Key Stage 2 English writing tests and marking. Good summative assessment should have a desirable impact, or wash back, because teachers generally spend a great deal of time preparing their students to take tests and examinations.

However, much of the criticism of summative assessment stems not from the instruments themselves but the secondary uses to which they are put. When the outcomes of tests and examinations are used as accountability measures – the criteria used to judge, reward and/or punish teachers, schools and national programmes – then unintended consequences often result. Teachers might spend too much time preparing children for tests at the expense of other curricular goals; undue attention and resources might be spent on children who are on the borderline of passing or reaching a particular threshold; **awarding bodies** might try to make examinations more accessible so that more students pass; markers might give the benefit of the doubt when deciding where a cut-score should be put; and in rare cases, teachers and administrators might actually cheat (Koretz, 2008). Inevitably test scores rise, even when other measures provide evidence that those increases do not reflect actual increased proficiency, for example in the USA NAEP scores have been reasonably flat even though the outcomes of state tests rise year on year.

Goodhart's (1975) law states that when a measure becomes a target, it ceases to be a good measure, and in cultures that rely on targets, such as in England with Key Stage 2 tests and GCSEs or in the USA through the No Child Left Behind legislation, people start questioning the tests themselves when actually it is the accountability system that is at fault. Almost everyone in the educational testing profession argues that the outcomes of one set of assessments should not be the sole judgement factor of any educational process, but **assessment policy** makers often ignore this argument. This has resulted in a shift from using tests as measurement instruments designed to provide information on students' achievements to using tests as policy instruments.

This is unfortunate, because there is evidence that used properly, test scores can have a positive effect. Chapman and Snyder (2000) argue that education officials can use test scores to target educational resources to low achieving schools or geographic areas, and testing can be used to shape teachers' pedagogical practices in desirable ways, can motivate teachers to improve their teaching and give them information with which to target remediation. Koretz *et al.* (2001) found that testing can provoke teachers to work harder and more effectively. Both Linn (2000) and Wiliam (2010a) have put forward a number of suggestions to improve accountability systems to make them work for students, teachers and policy makers.

TEACHERS' SUMMATIVE JUDGEMENTS

Teachers' summative judgements are part of the assessment systems in Scandinavia, the USA, Canada and Australia, although they are less trusted in the UK. A carefully set-out summative assessment system could make better use of teachers' judgements through clarifying who will make the judgements and how, a robust system of **quality assurance** and quality control (**moderation**), provision of clear criteria and performance standards, access to well designed tasks, pre-service and ongoing in-service training (Assessment Reform Group, 2006; Daugherty, 2010).

THE RELATIONSHIP BETWEEN SUMMATIVE AND FORMATIVE ASSESSMENT

Newton (2007a) among others, has questioned whether summative and formative assessment are truly conceptually or even pragmatically distinct, a notion first put forward by Scriven in 1967 (Taras, 2005). There are no distinct assessment types that we can label either formative or summative, nor is the way of gathering evidence different between the two. Instead it is the way that evidence gathered is used – to support feedback or to make a summary judgement. Indeed, evidence intended for summative use can also be used formatively. The outcomes of tests can be used diagnostically; teachers can use the outcomes of key stage tests to gauge students' learning needs. Students can use past examination papers to model their own questions and mark schemes.

Harlen (2006) warns that there is a danger of mistaking frequently collected summative judgements, for example in attributing achievement levels to individual pieces of student work in English or frequent quizzes in mathematics, for evidence that can be used formatively, thus undermining genuine **assessment for learning.** Instead she argues that assessment systems should allow evidence that teachers gather both for formative and summative purposes, but that a distinction should remain so that the summative does not swallow up the formative.

Continuous assessment acts as a bridge between formative and summative assessment. If students, as part of their studies, produce gradually completed units, which are built up into a portfolio of assessment evidence, then this continuous assessment serves a dual purpose, both formative and summative. This allows students to learn from their feedback and take greater responsibility for their own learning and achievements. Simultaneously, teachers and tutors are assisted in tracking the progress of learners, rather than waiting for the end of the course to discover, summatively, how much learning has taken place.

The nature and role of **feedback** is crucial to the distinction between formative and summative assessment. Bias and trust are also important issues. It is a reasonable hypothesis that in countries such as the UK, where summative assessment is highly regarded, there is less trust in the judgements of teachers due to reasons including the perceived danger of bias, and more reliance on external regulators and awarding bodies. It is perhaps no accident that in countries such as Finland, where external examinations are almost unheard of, school teaching is a selective, highly qualified and highly paid occupation, with greater status than in the UK.

FURTHER READING

Chapman, D. W. and Snyder Jr, C. W. (2000). 'Can high stakes national testing improve instruction: reexamining conventional wisdom'. *International Journal of Educational Development*, 20 (6), 457–74.

Harlen, W. (2007). 'Meanings, processes and properties of assessment'. In W. Harlen (ed.), *Assessment of Learning* (pp. 11–23). London: Sage.

Assessment Policy

Governments create policies concerning assessment standards in the belief that assessment outcomes are a true measure of national educational achievement, and that a well-educated populace guarantees that the nation will be globally competitive.

In light of international competitiveness and a belief that an educated populace is the key to economic success, governments seek to improve the quality and outcomes of their education systems. They want both to influence and to reliably gauge how well individual students, teachers, localities, regions and the nation itself are performing against education policy objectives. Increasingly the measure used is some form of assessment outcome. Governments develop assessment policies in the belief that assessment outcomes, generally but not always achieved through tests, are the fairest and most objective measure of national achievement.

As Scott (2011) argues, many policy makers have come to believe that tests can be progressive, equitable, rational and reasonable and can be used as instruments for educational reform.

Testing can also be a quick fix, externally mandated, rapidly implemented and the results can be publicly reported (Linn, 2001). Politicians need to show positive outcomes of their 'new' assessment policies within the lifetime of an election result. To achieve these aims, they develop systems that attach rewards and sanctions – accountability measures – to the outcomes of their assessment policies. Politicians believe that such accountability systems provoke improvements in educational performance but they are also used to evaluate whether or not the programmes and policies are working, which means that testing becomes both a policy instrument and a tool to determine the effectiveness of that policy (Herman and Baker, 2009).

Broadfoot (1999) labelled this 'performativity' and stated that its assumptions had so come to dominate policy thinking that certain notions were unquestioned, such as:

- that decisions concerning curriculum (inputs), pedagogy (process) and assessment (outcomes) should be centralised
- that there are standards of 'quality' that can be objectively measured
- that it is necessary and desirable to assess institutional quality according to externally-defined 'performance indicators'
- that the punitive use of league tables and other publicly-shaming devices will help to drive up educational performance
- that assessment is a 'neutral' measuring instrument which only requires further technical developments to make it more effective. (Broadfoot, 1999: 4–5)

Referring to both the USA and the UK, Berlak (1999, quoted in Broadfoot, 1999) argued that:

> there are no signs that the rush of governments to impose more testing and ranking of students, educational institutions and teachers is diminishing. Indeed the inclination of elected officials is toward more public accountability, which in the US and the UK translates to greater use of mass administered, high-stakes testing and rankings. In both nations ... ratings and test scores play a determinate role in where and how individuals are educated and ultimately gain or fail to gain access to particular schools, jobs or professions. The justification for mandating measurement of results employing rankings and tests is that, while imperfect, they are the best if not the only basis for guaranteeing neutrality, and making fair and objective statements about the comparative worth and educational productivity of students, teachers and educational institutions. (Broadfoot, 1999: 13)

There has been a shift from using tests as measurement instruments designed to produce information to a reliance on tests to influence policy and instruction. When assessment systems become high stake, even those that might be useful monitors of educational success can lose much of their dependability and credibility. The unintended negative effects of high-stakes accountability uses often outweigh the intended positive effects. This phenomenon is commonly known as Goodhart's Law in the UK and Campbell's Law in the USA. Succinctly, it states that when a measure becomes a target, it ceases to be a good measure.

Accountability policies force schools to shift away from a curriculum to a test focus, with students endlessly practising on old tests; what is not tested is either not taught or is given minimal time. Inevitably students on the cusp of passing or achieving a certain level are targeted for coaching. Both student and teacher motivation can be affected, since there is so much pressure on both to do well. There is also a danger that test scores will suffer from inflation, where increases in scores do not necessarily mean increased proficiency. In the USA individual states have shown year on year improvements in high-stakes standardised tests, but their results on the National Assessment of Educational Progress (NAEP), which uses sampling and is low stakes, remain pretty steady (Koretz, 2008).

Despite calls to rely more on teacher judgement, it is unlikely that accountability-based assessment policy will disappear any time soon. Therefore critics have called for better accountability system design.

Baker and Linn (2002) developed standards for accountability systems, including:

- Accountability systems should employ different types of data from multiple sources.
- Accountability systems should include data elements that allow for interpretations of student, institution, and administrative performance.
- Accountability expectations should be made public and understandable for all participants in the system.
- Decisions about individual students should not be made on the basis of a single test.
- The validity of measures that have been administered as part of an accountability system should be documented for the various purposes of the system.
- If tests are to help improve system performance, data should be provided illustrating that the results are modifiable by quality instruction and student effort.
- If test data are used as a basis of rewards or sanctions, evidence of technical quality of the measures and error rates associated with misclassification of individuals or institutions should be published.
- If tests are claimed to measure content and performance standards, evidence of the relationship to particular standards or sets of standards should be provided.
- System results should be made broadly available to the press, with sufficient time for reasonable analysis and with clear explanations of legitimate and potential illegitimate interpretations of results. (Baker and Linn, 2002: 19–24)

FURTHER READING

Broadfoot, P. (1999). *Empowerment or performativity? English assessment policy in the late twentieth century*. Paper presented at the Assessment Reform Group Symposium on Assessment Policy at the British Educational Research Association annual conference, Brighton, University of Sussex.

Herman, J. L. and Baker, E. L. (2009). 'Assessment policy: making sense of the Babel'. In G. Sykes, B. L. Schneider, D. N. Plank and T. G. Ford (eds), *Handbook of Education Policy Research*. London: Routledge.

Scott, D. (2011) 'Assessment reform: High-stakes testing and knowing the contents of other minds'. *Assessment Reform in Education, Education in the Asia-Pacific Region: Issues, Concerns and Prospects*, 14 (2), 155–63.

ASSESSING APTITUDE (ABILITY) AND ATTAINMENT (ACHIEVEMENT)

Aptitude is the capability and potential of a person to develop skills or acquire knowledge. Aptitude assessment is meant to measure a person's cognitive skills, ability to learn and the speed of that learning. Attainment (or achievement) pertains to accomplishment – what someone knows and is able to do. There is not a strict line dividing aptitude and attainment tests and assessments.

In public controversies about tests, disputants have failed to recognize that virtually every bit of evidence obtained with IQs would be approximately duplicated if the same study were carried out with a comprehensive measure of achievement. (Cronbach, 1976: 211)

WHAT IS APTITUDE AND WHY ASSESS IT?

Aptitude pertains to a person's capability and potential to develop skills or acquire knowledge. Commonly associated with general intelligence, aptitude is perceived of as a set of stable, fixed and heritable traits. Testing for aptitude has a long history dating back to Chinese Civil Service **examinations** (see **Intelligence Quotient**). More modern examples are England's 11+ test and UK medical and dental school tests. American students take SAT tests, which measure verbal, mathematical and writing ability not associated with particular curriculum or subject standards.

The 11+'s underlying premise was that while secondary schooling should be available to all children, those children's needs could best be met by differentiated provision (secondary modern, technical and grammar schools) based on ability. The person most closely associated with this testing system, Sir Cyril Burt, believed in a fixed concept of general ability and that this ability could be reliably measured (Coldron *et al.*, 2009).

Aptitude testing is meant to measure a person's cognitive skills, ability to learn and the speed of that learning. Test results are used to predict future success – for the 11+ it was success in secondary schools; for the US SATs success at university. They attempt to minimise influences such as language, culture and educational experiences by using tasks that look different from the usual school learning requirements, for example in testing abstract reasoning, non-verbal reasoning, problem solving and/ or spatial relationships (Reynolds *et al.*, 2005).

WHAT IS ATTAINMENT AND WHY ASSESS IT?

Attainment (or achievement) pertains to accomplishment – what someone knows and is able to do. In educational assessment, attainment is associated with how well students did upon the completion of a course of study or on subject-based tests. This model assumes that training and education can improve people's achievement outcomes. National Curriculum tests, GCSE and A level examinations are examples of English and Welsh high-profile attainment tests. In the US, No Child Left Behind tests set out to measure students' basic skills, the National Assessment of Educational Progress (NAEP) tests sample student achievement in various curriculum areas and the Advanced Placement (AP) programme culminates in curriculum-based examinations geared toward the highest achievers. The French Baccalaureate and German Abitur are both achievement examinations and examples can be found, either nationally or classroom-based in most nations. TIMSS and PIRLS are attainment tests; PISA combines elements of attainment and aptitude (see **international assessment**).

Attainment tests contain curriculum specific questions. It is posited that future learning depends to some extent on past learning, so doing well on attainment tests provides evidence of future success (Izard, 2005). Attainment tests can be developed and used by teachers or by external organisations and used in national testing programmes. Workplace attainment tests are also common, through vocational and occupational qualifications and in everyday setting such as driving tests. Attainment tests can be **norm-referenced** or **criterion-referenced** (National Foundation for Educational Research, n.d.).

Attainment tests can track student achievement over time, compare group achievement across classes and/or schools, be used in high-stakes decision making, gauge the strengths and weaknesses of students and ascertain instructional programme effectiveness.

THE RELATIONSHIP OF APTITUDE AND ATTAINMENT

There is no strict line dividing the two types of tests. Miller *et al.*, citing Cronbach, explain that the two types of testing are actually on a continuum from content-oriented attainment tests to attainment tests of general education, school-oriented aptitude tests, culture-oriented verbal aptitude tests and culture-oriented nonverbal aptitude tests (Miller *et al.*, 2009).

Controversy arises around which type of test predicts future performance. Aptitude tests are prospective; attainment tests retrospective. Attainment tests cannot always infer ability directly – test takers may not adequately show what they know on the day. Aptitude tests try to test general ability without relying on what the test taker has already learned, which Burt believed fairer to students who had not had equal opportunities to learn (Coldron *et al.*, 2009).

However, the pendulum has largely swung in favour of those who believe that past achievement is often the best predictor of future achievement, with curriculum-based tests as better predictors of success in those subjects, and more general attainment tests – basic skills, application of principles and interpretation of data – as better predictors of overall future attainment (Miller *et al.*, 2009).

Opportunity to learn affects outcomes, as evidenced by studies done about why UK private school students with equivalent A level grades to state school students do worse at university. Ogg *et al.* found that private school students' performance at Oxford University correlated to their scores on an aptitude test, i.e. their excellent A level grades were due, in part, to superior school effects (Ogg *et al.*, 2009). These sorts of factors have led some to argue that, at least for university admissions purposes, both aptitude and achievement tests should factor into decisions.

FURTHER READING

Coldron, J., Willis, B. and Wolstenholme, C. (2009). 'Selection by Attainment and aptitude in English Secondary Schools'. *British Journal of Educational Studies*, 57 (3), 245–64.

Jencks, C. and Phillips, M. (1999). 'Aptitude or achievement: why do test scores predict Educational Attainment and Earnings?'. In S. E. Mayer and P. E. Peterson (eds), *Earning and Learning: How Schools Matter*. Washington, DC: Brookings Institution Press.

attainment

> Awarding bodies, also known as awarding organisations and examination boards, are the institutions responsible for developing and awarding the qualifications that are used in schools, colleges and the workplace.

Awarding bodies design **qualifications** and their attendant assessments and subsequently administer and award on those assessments, which can consist of workplace-based activities, **coursework**, controlled assessment, tests and **examinations**. Awarding bodies in the UK are subject to **regulation**. In England, the regulator is the Office of Qualifications and Examinations Regulation (Ofqual). Currently, the government will not fund schools and colleges to offer qualifications that Ofqual has not accredited. There are 178 awarding organisations; six of them are the main providers of qualifications for 14- to 19-year-olds (Ofqual, 2012b). This entry concentrates on them; they are the Assessment and Qualifications Alliance (AQA), the Council for the Curriculum Examinations and Assessment (CCEA), City & Guilds, Edexcel/Pearson, Oxford, Cambridge and RSA (OCR) and the Welsh Joint Education Committee (WJEC). CCEA and WJEC are based in Northern Ireland and Wales respectively.

Universities created the first academic examinations boards in the late 19th century. Vocationally oriented awarding bodies, such as City & Guilds, have their origins in the crafts and guilds systems. Schools and colleges historically have had the choice of which awarding body to use but prior to the late 20th century choice was largely regionally based. In 1953, shortly after students sat the first A and O levels, there were 10 academic awarding bodies. From 1965 to 1988, a number of additional awarding bodies offered Certificates of Secondary Education (CSE), which were aimed at students who were not going to take O levels. When O levels and CSEs merged in 1988 to create GCSEs, the CSE awarding bodies became part of the larger examining groups. By the mid-1990s, academic awarding bodies merged into the five unitary bodies extant today. Those bodies have expanded their provision beyond

key concepts in educational assessment

GCSEs and A levels to offer vocationally related qualifications as well (Tattersall, 2007).

Because there is more than one awarding body for A levels and GCSEs, the government has put a regulatory system in place to ensure that they maintain qualifications and assessment standards across examination papers in different series, specifications in the same subject, specifications in different subjects, between awarding bodies and over time. It is Ofqual's responsibility to ensure that awarding bodies have satisfactory administrative, financial and human resource systems in place, and that they are held to account for their performance. To do so, Ofqual monitors standards in qualifications, examinations and tests and reports its findings publicly (Ofqual, 2011).

Awarding bodies' qualifications are governed by regulatory codes of practice. The codes' aims are to promote quality, consistency, accuracy and **fairness** in assessment and awarding, as well as to help maintain standards. To achieve this, the codes set out the principles and practice for the assessment and **quality assurance** of qualifications; the roles and responsibilities of awarding bodies and their personnel and of centres; the requirements for awarding bodies in preparing question papers, tasks and **mark schemes**; **standardising** marking (both external and internal); the awarding process including awarding, marking review, maintaining an archive and issuing results; rules regarding candidates with particular requirements; and how to deal with malpractice and appeals (Ofqual, 2011).

Tattersall (2007) argues that awarding bodies' powers have been eroded through the increasing use of criteria, codes of practice, and monitoring. State control through awarding body regulation presumes that government can be both effective and impartial, but as Wolf (2009) argues, it can actually stifle genuine reform and innovation through 'regulatory capture' in which the mutual self-interest of government, regulators and awarding bodies reduces competition and incentives to innovate. And because government measures its success through the performance of these agencies, it has a strong incentive to control, as much as possible, their output.

FURTHER READING

Isaacs, T. (2010). 'Educational assessment in England'. *Assessment in Education: Principles, Policy & Practice*, 17 (3), 315–34.

Oates, T. (2009). *The Cambridge Approach: Principles for Designing, Administering and Evaluating Assessment*. Cambridge: Cambridge Assessment.

Basic Skills Assessment

> Basic Skills are also referred to as Skills For Life, essential skills, core skills, key skills or functional skills. In the UK, these include adult literacy, numeracy and spoken language, English for Speakers of Other Languages (ESOL) and ICT skills. Assessment tools and approaches range from the diagnostic to summative national tests.

This key concept, and by implication, what is to be assessed, has been variously redefined and re-designated over the past decade or so. While the pursuit of literacy and numeracy starts from early years and continues through to adult education, the core focus here relates to the development of abilities, knowledge and understanding which adults (sometimes including young people from 16+) are deemed to need in order to 'function' in society and in employment. Skills that are considered basic and on whose terms are subject to shifting perceptions in academic and political discourse and in adult literacy as a social practice (Papen, 2005). Re-evaluation of the basic skills that enable people to function economically and socially, and to what level it is required they attain them, further stimulate change in policy and terminology. The modification of what are considered to be basic skills can also be attributed to the fast changing nature of the economy. Basic ICT skills in 2000, for instance, were quite different from basic ICT skills in 2012. This is due to generational developments in the technological tools and the issues and problems to which they must be applied and this varies considerably from region to region across the globe. Decisive factors are the particular economic conditions and technological infrastructure of the region in question and education, vocational training and/or lifelong learning policy.

Experts and providers hold different views on the most appropriate methodology for identifying those in need of basic or Skills For Life

key concepts in educational assessment

assessments, and even more so, on the most appropriate response. There is a debate as to whether, in practice, particular kinds of skills are best taught in a discrete context in basic skills classes or by being embedded in learning that has a broader purpose such as within vocational qualifications. Karen Taylor, Director of Literacy, Language and Numeracy, and the Workplace at the National Institute of Adult Continuing Education (NIACE), believes that 'adults don't willingly join a class to improve their basic skills ... they usually get there by a much more circuitous route – through a "leisure class" ... or the sheer hard work of a Trade Union Learning Rep' (Ethos, 2008: 1).

Specialist **diagnostic**-type assessment tools have been devised to test basic skills in adults. These have been designed to help adult learners and their teachers and, where appropriate, learners' employers, ascertain general skill levels and/or the desirability for further diagnostic assessment. They are also designed to give the government information about current skills levels in the country and they offer a benchmark from which to set achievement targets. Other assessment tools have been designed to determine an individual's potential need, but not to indicate his or her specific level.

In the UK, the order in which different stages of basic skills assessments take place starts with screening. Screening involves what have been termed Skills Check Tools. These have been designed to determine an individual's potential but they do not indicate his or her specific level. They are followed by Initial Assessment Tools that have been developed to help learners and their teachers ascertain general skill levels and/or the desirability for further diagnostic assessment. Diagnostic assessment may then take place if particular traits and attributes have been identified that merit further analysis to provide more detailed information about how these can best be addressed. Examples of these would be tests for dyslexia, hearing loss and sight impairment. All of the above can be termed preparatory assessments enabling learner and provider to ensure that the particular course of study is both appropriate and properly resourced. Teachers and sometimes technicians should be informed of the specific requirements of their learners so that they can adapt their teaching strategy and environment accordingly and undertake any necessary training themselves.

In the 2001 Skills for Life strategy (DfEE, 2001) it was hoped that tutors would promote formal summative assessment since it was considered that every student had the right to obtain a recognised qualification. By 2010, following a strategy update (DIUS, 2009), funded provision was predominantly accredited and summative assessments in the form of national tests at levels 1 or 2 were to be administered at the end of a stage or course of learning. In certain cases these might be taken on a week-by-week basis. They cover subjects such as: Application of Number and Adult Numeracy; Communication, Adult Literacy and ESOL Skills for Life Reading; and Information and Communication Technologies. Many of these have been produced, by City & Guilds for example, as online tests and tend to be multiple-choice in design.

The overarching purpose of these national summative tests is one of accountability (Ecclestone, 2010). At government level they enable claims to be made about the raising of literacy and numeracy levels within the adult population. At provider level they allow learning providers to claim or account for funding of provision by the government. The emphasis on summative tests can distort the focus from the support of learner development to demonstration of the ability to get learners to pass these tests. One consequence of this is that the overall results are unlikely to produce an entirely accurate picture of the extent to which adults have genuinely enhanced their ability to use such skills in ways that are important and meaningful to them. In 1997 the UK Labour Government set the strategy behind this shift in focus and purpose of assessment for basic skills. It was at this time that the principal purpose became one of accountability. Governments may want to be seen to have met or even exceeded their targets but the adults whose attainment is being counted may not have acquired the extent, degree or level of learning claimed nor the kind of learning that they most desire or need.

Functional skills in the wider further education context of 14–19 qualifications and apprenticeships have produced much harder and more complex assessments because they are applied to facilitate problem solving. Examples of assessment design and tools can be found at http://www.excellence.qia.org.uk/functionalskills. Over 3000 centres participated in the piloting of these qualifications between 2007 and 2010. Functional skills assessments must provide realistic contexts, scenarios and problems, specify tasks that are relevant to the context, require applications of knowledge, skills and understanding for a purpose, require problem solving and assess process skills and the outcome of their application in different contexts (DfE, 2011a). Unlike basic skills testing, these assessments include open-ended questions that require extended writing.

FURTHER READING

Department for Innovation Universities and Skills (DIUS) (2009). *Skills for Life: Changing Lives.* London.

Ecclestone, K. (2010). *Transforming Formative Assessment in Lifelong Learning.* London: McGraw-Hill.

Comparability

In order to put forward sound, equitable and fair judgements about students' achievements across assessments and examinations, syllabuses, subjects and over time, assessment experts have tried to develop concepts, methods and techniques to deliver comparable assessment standards. This is to ensure that those in a position to make judgements about progression, selection and employment treat different students with different educational profiles and from different years, as equally as possible.

D. Royce Sadler (1995) posited that there were two broad notions of comparability: the ability to compare one assessment to another; and that the assessments being compared *are* equivalent to each other. In the first, the question is whether two things that are different from each other *can* be compared; in the second the question is whether those two different things are 'more or less equal' (Sadler, 1995: 2). In order to ascertain the latter you have to have the former.

WHY SEEK COMPARABILITY?

Comparability issues have political and social significance and can directly affect students' life chances. For example, in most countries university entrance depends on how well applicants have done in the subjects they studied – if grades in those subjects (and the subjects themselves) are not comparable then students, their parents and the public would presumably be concerned about the **fairness** of admission decisions. Students' results on **examinations** are used to judge not only the students themselves, but their teachers, their schools or colleges, their local education authority and national performance (see **assessment policy**).

Comparability is an international concern, especially during the transition from secondary to higher education (Lamprianou, 2009), with some countries adjusting students' examination results in an attempt to ensure fairness. For example, in some parts of Australia, where higher education applicants are rank ordered, subject outcomes are adjusted through statistical formulae in order to ensure comparability, so that students will not be penalised for taking difficult subjects.

At its most basic, comparability is about fairness: making sure that different students, with different educational profiles, from different years are treated as equally as possible by those in a position to make judgements about progression, selection and employment.

WHAT TO COMPARE

We look for comparability, defined as the application of the same standard across different assessments:

- of judgements across the same assessment tasks marked by different people, for example **coursework**
- within different versions of assessments, for example two examinations in the same subject given at separate times
- between specifications in the same subject, for example from a number of providers or **awarding bodies**
- across subjects, for example physics and French
- across time, that is over a period of years, even decades.

In the context of England, where Desmond Nuttall (cited in Newton, 2007b: 9) proclaimed comparability to be a disease, this could mean proving that a grade C in one awarding body's foundation (lower) tier mathematics GCSE examination was the equivalent of another awarding body's grade C in a higher tier English Literature GCSE examination.

If an A is an A is an A, then is it fair that in the summer of 2010 16.3% of students got an A or A* in A level Computing, while 44.8% of their peers got an A or A* in A level Mathematics? To try to answer that question it is necessary to look more closely at comparability methods and techniques and their underlying assumptions.

HOW TO COMPARE

There is no one technique for achieving comparability that most assessment experts agree should be used. Different experts use different terminology for describing very similar comparability concepts (see Newton, 2010: 287 for a table listing alternative comparability schemes from 1981 onwards). Using Baird's (2007) terminology, which most assessment experts would recognise even if they use different terminology, it is possible to look at some of the common conceptions of comparability.

Cohort referencing

In this method the same proportion of students are given certain grades each year. For example, until the 1980s A level pass rates were kept similar across subjects. With cohort referencing there is no possibility for grade inflation – no matter how well or badly students do in a given year, 10% of them will get As, 20% Bs, etc. The benefit of this system is that it is simple for awarding bodies to administer and for the public to understand. However, it means that differences in attainment across cohorts from year to year, subject to subject, specification to specification, examination to examination are not taken into account. If mathematics attracts students of higher ability than computing, would it be fair that 10% of each group got grade As? Baird (2007) argues that in this type of system high-achieving students would start taking subjects that had in the past been taken by weaker students in order to maximise their chances of getting a good grade, and teachers would seek out the 'easiest' specification in a subject, again to increase the chances that their students would get good grades.

Catch-all definition

Cresswell (1996) put forward this definition, which states that students of the same characteristics (general ability, socio-economic class, conscientiousness, etc.) would be awarded the same grade on average on whichever examination they entered. Statistical solutions are generally used to determine examination standards here. This conception seems to be common sense, but putting it into practice is quite difficult. What factors would be included in trying to define the 'same characteristics'? How would those who have to make assessment decisions get access to the information? Would it be desirable to weight the information; that is, is socio-economic background more or less important than how well the student was taught?

Criterion referencing

In this conception, which is heavily used in assessments that rely on internal or teacher judgements, a student's work is judged against a fixed performance standard – known in the UK as criteria, and in the USA as rubrics. In this scheme there is no limit to how many students can achieve a certain grade – the determinant is whether or not they have demonstrated that they have fulfilled the criteria. Writing usable criteria is very difficult and they are subject to examiners' and markers' interpretation.

Some **criterion-referenced** assessment systems insist that students fulfil all criteria (mastery model); others allow compensation, where stronger performance on some criteria can counterbalance weaker performance on others. This counterbalancing distinguishes strong from weak criterion referencing (see below).

Weak criterion referencing

Weak criterion referencing uses both statistical information and examiners' judgement and is the most common form of judging examination standards in the UK. It allows examiners to set grades using criterion-referenced judgements, but also takes into account statistical information such as students' past performance and the proportion of students gaining particular grades in the past. Over the past decade in the UK, the statistical element has gained in importance, the assumption being that students' general abilities do not vary that dramatically from year to year, so adjusting grade boundaries to achieve year-on year comparability is fair.

COMMON TECHNIQUES FOR MEASURING COMPARABILITY

Even tests that are built to measure exactly the same ability (for example, spelling) in exactly the same way (for example, with a 20 mark test) may end up being slightly different in terms of the overall difficulty of questions for students (for example, one or two words turning out to be harder than the test authors anticipated on test 2). In order to ensure comparability across the tests the cut-off scores (how many marks a student needs to get a particular grade or level) may need to be adjusted from one year to the next. Common boundary setting techniques include:

Angoff/Bookmark

- where experts judge the difficulty of individual questions for each test separately. These techniques rely on experts having a 'typical' student in mind and using their judgement about whether or not that student would answer a question correctly. Without actual student work, this can be a guessing game.

Script scrutiny

- where experts judge the quality of students' performances (at different marks) across old and new tests and ascertain at which mark (on the new test) they find the same quality of performance as at the cut-off score (on the old test).

Equating

- where both old and new versions of the test are linked either on a matched sample of students (as in the National Curriculum tests in England) or a matched sample of items (as in the US SATs) to ascertain, on average, how much higher or lower students might score on the new test. In US SATs, students answer questions in an equating section that is not included in their scores but is used in the development of future tests. The key here is that test takers do not know which the equating section is. If separate tests on the same students are used, as the anchoring tests for the National Curriculum tests are in England, test takers might take the live test more seriously than the anchor, leading to different levels of performance.

None of the techniques and methods employed to gauge comparability is without flaws, and Sadler (1995) argued that if we stopped pretending that different subjects could be made comparable then all users would have to become thoroughly grounded in the distinctive contribution each subject made and not even try to equate them.

Coe, R. (2010). 'Understanding comparability of examination standards'. *Research Papers in Education*, 25 (3), 271–84.

Newton, P., Baird, J. A., Goldstein, H., Patrick, H. and Tymms, P. (eds). (2007). *Techniques for Monitoring the Comparability of Examination Standards*. London: QCA.

Schools Council (1979). 'Standards in public examinations: problems and possibilities'. *Occasional Paper*, 1, London: London Schools Council.

Continuous Assessment

Continuous assessment is a classroom strategy implemented by teachers, lecturers or trainers to determine the knowledge, understanding, and skills attained by learners. Professionals administer assessments in a variety of ways over time to allow them to observe multiple tasks and to collect evidence about what learners know, understand and can do. Learners receive feedback from staff based on their performance that allows them to focus on topics they have not yet fully mastered.

Teachers learn which learners need further support and remediation and which learners are ready to move on to more complex work. Thus, the results of the assessments help to ensure that all learners make progress throughout the school or college cycle, thereby increasing their academic achievement.

In continuous assessment, teachers, lecturers and trainers assess the curriculum as implemented in the classroom, the workshop or the learning environment. It also allows these professionals to evaluate the effectiveness of their teaching strategies relative to the curriculum, and to change those strategies as suggested by their learners' responses. Additionally, continuous assessments provide information on achievement of particular levels of skills, understanding and knowledge rather than the achievement of marks or scores. Consequently, continuous assessment enables learners to monitor their achievement of personal goals and to understand their progress towards those goals before it is too late to achieve them. Continuous assessment can also incorporate **peer assessment** easily as part of ongoing procedures rather than as a bolt-on to current practice.

The benefits of continuous assessment are numerous. Such an approach to assessment allows the teacher to use a variety of assessment instruments, such as rich tasks, projects and portfolios to gain a much richer understanding of a learner's capabilities and is not reliant on a single end-of-session test that may disadvantage a particular learner. Teaching staff can collect evidence relating to the cognitive, affective and psychomotor domains of their learners; this is not often possible in a single assessment. Continuous assessment can also provide not only a holistic approach to assessment, but also immediate and effective **feedback** to both the learner and to the practitioner about a learner's strengths and areas that need further development. As such, continuous assessment can be used as an effective **diagnostic** tool. It allows teaching staff to monitor the effectiveness of their own teaching and pedagogy, giving an insight into what learners have assimilated during a teaching session and what they still need to do, or indeed what the teacher still needs to cover or present in a different format.

To be successful, continuous assessment needs to follow a carefully orchestrated approach. This can be summarised as follows and is closely linked to **Assessment for Learning (AfL)**:

1 Ensure that learning outcomes are carefully stated, negotiated and agreed with the learners and made explicit.
2 Ensure that the assessment criteria are understood by all those who will be assessed. These too need to be made explicit and understood by the learners. They need to understand what success looks like before they are assessed. Ensuring that the assessment criteria are understood by all those involved helps practitioners to introduce peer assessment when it is thought helpful.
3 Ensure that feedback is carefully phrased to the individual learner, concentrating on the learner's performance of the task and couched in the language of the intended learning outcomes as well as the agreed assessment criteria.

As Eraut (2004: 201) pointed out, 'Learning is "A significant change in capability or understanding." *This excludes*: the acquisition of further information when it does not contribute to such changes.' Thus effective continuous assessment must add to the acquisition of further information and, as Stobart (2009) commented, 'learning is most effective when it builds on what we already know, makes sense to the learner and is active and social (unpaginated video presentation).' Effective continuous assessment ensures that these preconditions take place.

The disadvantages of continuous assessment have also been well documented (Richardson, 2003). Such an approach to assessment requires a commitment from all staff to the implementation of the approach in an agreed format. Setting up such a system can prove labour-intensive and time-consuming. Senior management within a school, college or workplace must support the implementation of the procedures, setting aside time for practitioners to **standardise** and to **moderate** the assessments. New staff entering the institution need to follow a planned induction programme so that practice is consistent across the institution or at least across the subject area. Continuous assessment is also open to plagiarism by learners, so vigilance on the part of the teacher, lecturer or tutor is of paramount importance. Staff need to be skilled users of a variety of assessment instruments, skilled interpreters of the evidence that is generated and skilled recorders of that data. It is usual for the data to be collected in a consistent format. Again, staff may need training in the use and implementation of such systems.

Continuous assessment is not usually used for high-stakes assessment; rather it is an approach to teaching and learning that incorporates assessment at the heart of the process. This highlights another disadvantage relating to continuous assessment in that learners may feel continuously under the microscope, which can damage the relationship between teacher and learner. Without very careful planning, continuous assessment can result in learners being over-assessed. Access to resources may not be equitable, giving some learners an advantage over their less affluent peers. This needs to be taken into consideration if such an approach is to be adopted.

One form of introducing continuous assessment into the English curriculum was developed through the Assessing Pupils' Progress (APP) programme. This has been well documented and evaluated by external agencies across a number of schools in England during the first decade of the 21st century. The Office for Standards in Education, Children's Services and Skills (Ofsted, 2011) found that APP helped strengthen assessment practices, improving teachers' understanding of students' attainment and progress when linked with identifying and explaining objectives, questioning students and giving feedback. When successfully implemented – and the report admitted that APP implementation was not always successful – teachers adapted and expanded their approaches to assessment. Detractors have criticised APP for increasing workload and encouraging criteria compliance through asking teachers to tick off formally during the course of the year when students have reached certain attainment levels (Barker, 2010). Both supporters and critics concede that in order to work, continuous assessment such as APP needs to be supported by teacher training.

FURTHER READING

Chartered Institute of Educational Assessors (CIEA) (2007). *Teacher Assessment.* Available at: http://www.ciea.co.uk

Department for Children, Schools and Families (DCSF) (2008). The Assessment for Learning Strategy. London: DCSF.

Richardson, C. (ed.) (2003). *Whither Assessment?* London: QCA.

Coursework

Coursework is oral, written work and presentations integrated into both learning activities and assessment tasks.

Coursework is generally understood as a task or activity where work is assigned by a teacher or instructor, completed by the student during the course of study, within a set timescale and assessed as part of the entire course. Coursework is usually assessed as part of the student's grade in the course and is associated with **continuous assessment** as a means of delivering a student-centred curriculum. This can occur as a mix of **oral** and **peer assessment** as well as written work or group tasks linked to an awarding organisation's controlled assessment task. A controlled assessment task is one where the student carries out the work, but, for part of the task, in conditions that are 'controlled' or monitored carefully by teachers. The regulations governing this type of assessment vary according to subject domain and educational context, but they must be followed if the assessment is to be seen as **valid**.

Coursework and controlled assessment are often referred to as internal assessment. In England, the amount of internal assessment differs from subject to subject and from one qualification type to the next. Generally, the more applied and skills-based the curriculum is, the more internal assessment will be found. Sometimes a qualification will contain no coursework – GCSE mathematics is an example; sometimes a qualification will be 100% internally assessed – as is often the case with occupational qualifications. Concerns about students cutting and pasting information from the internet or buying coursework outright, inappropriate parental help and variations in the number of drafts teachers read and the guidance given on those drafts caused the shift from more flexibly managed coursework to strictly regulated controlled assessment. In *Education by Numbers*, Mansell (2007) claimed that teachers coached their students through coursework essays, providing them with writing frameworks that guided them through structure, headings and topics. Mansell accused some teachers of deliberately giving students good grades on their coursework in order to improve their school's position on performance tables. For some critics, even introducing tighter controls does not go far enough and they advocate introducing 100% externally marked, end-of-course examinations for high-stakes qualifications such as GCSEs and A levels.

However, curricula have been designed and delivered that include coursework because many educators and educational theorists believe that student-centred learning is highly motivating. Through such hands-on activity the curriculum content and assessment methodology become embedded as meaningful experiential learning. This concept of coursework operating as activity-based learning builds upon John Dewey's (1938) original learning theories. He claimed that learning is situated and knowledge constructed by the participating learner.

From this concept, meaningful formative assessment tasks linked to student **feedback** can be developed that can be implemented as part of an **assessment for learning** strategy. According to Clarke (2005) and others, it is the effectiveness of the feedback, linked to the learning objectives, that maximises the impact upon learners and thereby on learners' outcomes. Consequently, many educationalists adopt such strategies, which generally include innovative types of coursework as a form of task-based and situated learning experience. Such imaginative tasks can cut across subject domains, for example designing an electronic toy as part of an engineering project can also include elements of mathematics, English and business studies. Coursework can also be used to assess project work and other kinds of **work-based assessment** and this can be completed either individually or as part of a team-building activity.

Much of **vocational assessment** relies upon a component of coursework that is linked to project work tasks covered by a system of **group assessment** requiring local **moderation** and **internal verification** of results achieved. Coursework designed to operate in such a context can be linked to ICT activities in the form of e-learning courseware resources hosted on virtual learning environments (VLEs) that can in turn offer **e-assessment** opportunities.

Although controlled assignments have superseded coursework in much of the UK's assessment regimes in high-stakes subject-based examinations, internationally this is not the case, with South Africa, Australia and the USA still allowing coursework projects as part of their high-stakes assessment.

FURTHER READING

Black, P. J., Harrison, C., Lee, C., Marshall, B. and Wiliam, D. (2003). *Assessment for Learning: Putting it into Practice*. Milton Keynes: Open University Press.

Magennis, S. and Farrell, A. (2005). 'Teaching and Learning Activities: expanding the repertoire to support student learning'. In G. O'Neill, S. Moore and B. McMullin (eds), *Emerging Issues in the Practice of University Learning and Teaching*. Dublin: All Ireland Society for Higher Education, Higher Education Authority.

coursework

Criterion Referencing

> The individual's understanding of specific subject matter is evaluated against pre-specified criteria. The outcome is judged on the student's own performance and not with reference to performance by others.

A criterion-referenced assessment is where criteria are specified for learner performance at different levels. Learners who show that they have demonstrated competence in each of the criteria achieve success in the domain being assessed, regardless of the performance of others similarly assessed.

Criterion-referenced scores are sometimes referred to as levels, which may be defined in terms of specific competencies that are expected of learners. It is usually compared and contrasted with **norm referencing**. The 'norms' in norm referencing refer to average, below and above average performance. These are derived from a particular population type and from the typical range of scores one might expect that population type (a year group or key stage, for instance) to deliver in an assessment.

Criterion referencing, by contrast, is derived from an external set of standards for attitudes, behaviours, skills or particular knowledge and understanding. These standards may refer to occupation-related attributes, employment-related performance or knowledge and/or skill-sets in an educational domain. Competence-based qualifications offer a classic example of criterion-referenced assessment design (although see the critical note on this in entry on norm referencing). As the significance of passing a criterion-based assessment implies ability at or competence in a particular level then the design of the assessment tool, task or test requires particular and precise attention to be paid to the items and constructs. These must be detailed so that they offer specific and appropriate coverage of the skills and attributes being assessed.

key concepts in
educational assessment

The extent to which such an assessment requires all as opposed to most (80% or 90%, say) of the criteria to be successfully passed depends on the social or professional significance of the assessment and the public requirement for reassurance that those who have passed are safe to practise (if appropriate) or dependable to a specific desirable standard in the public eye. The driving test represents a much-quoted example of a criterion-based assessment where a very high percentage of criteria, including some non-negotiable ones, must be achieved.

Criterion-referenced scores, then, are used to distinguish between those who have and those who have not acquired the abilities necessary to undertake a particular kind of performance satisfactorily. There are also instances where the scoring system is both norm- and criterion-referenced. That is to say, an assessment in which a candidate is required to pass all or most specified elements but in which it is also possible to gain a distinction, merit, pass or fail. An example would be an examination for a musical instrument where ability assessed includes sight reading, aural skills, instrument-playing technique and musical interpretation. A trickier example is that of current A levels, which changed from largely norm-referenced (or cohort-referenced) to criterion-referenced but where the final attribution of grades is still influenced by normative expectations.

The merits of criterion-referenced scores include their potential 'to distinguish between those who have or have not developed the knowledge, skills or abilities required for a specific activity' or field (Anastasi, 1988, cited in Coaley, 2010: 64). They are employed in education where a framework of prescribed standards determines students' achievements as being at a particular level or not. The underlying assumption in many contemporary areas of criterion-referenced assessment, such as National Vocational Qualifications (NVQ) in the UK, many of the 14–19 qualifications, and national curriculum assessment, is that the majority of those being assessed will be deemed satisfactory (competent). The minority who are not-yet-competent will require additional education, work experience and/or training and development until they are.

Two major criticisms of criterion-referenced assessment, especially in vocational qualifications and in the workplace, relate to manageability and **reliability**. On the one hand, the gathering of portfolios of evidence can result in so much material that the assessor takes a tick-box approach to 'signing it off'. On the other, the presumed advantage of specificity of criteria aimed at making the process fairer does not prevent different assessors from interpreting the criteria differently. And criteria are notably difficult to specify; as Wiliam (1993: 341) stated, 'no criterion, no matter how precisely phrased, admits of an unambiguous interpretation'.

The limitations of criterion referencing are that the interpretation of scores is notoriously subjective, prone to bias and vulnerable to change. Bias might be related to several aspects of the assessment design itself (e.g. lack of item/construct rigour), or the marking process by the assessors marking the assessment (e.g. marker bias not thoroughly moderated, including grade-related or weighting bias where markers consciously or unconsciously elevate one criterion over another). Bias can also arise due to the conditions under which the assessment was taken by candidates – such as unanticipated interruption or extraneous noise – affecting reliability in norm-referenced assessment.

A different kind of limitation of criterion referencing relates to the fact that the standards and criteria set, normally devised by those considered expert in the relevant domain, must inevitably change over time. This arises as further research, knowledge and understanding develop in that domain. To remain valid and reliable, any measuring tool needs to be adjusted accordingly. The danger is that the domain changes but assessment tools lag behind. Finally, if it is not also norm-referenced, an individual's achievement of a criterion-referenced award, of which competence-based assessment can be seen as a type (Wolf, 1995), says little about the quality of that achievement by comparison with 'peers'.

The relationship between criterion referencing and formative assessment has been much discussed, with most educationalists stressing that success criteria should always be shared with learners so that they know what is expected of them. Torrance (2007) warns, however, that this practice can lead to a culture of 'criteria compliance' (p. 282), where **assessment for learning** becomes assessment as learning, with increased teacher coaching and support to guide students on how to fulfil the criteria: 'transparency of objectives coupled with extensive use of coaching and practice to help learners meet them is in danger of removing the challenge of learning and reducing the quality and validity of outcomes achieved' (Torrance, 2007: 282) (see also **feedback**).

FURTHER READING

Rowntree, D. (1987). *Assessing students: How shall we know them?* London: Kogan Page.
Wolf, A. (1993). *Assessment Issues and Problems in a Criterion-based System*. London: Further Education Unit.
Wright, R. J. (2007). *Educational Assessment: Tests and Measurements in the Age of Accountability*. New York: Sage.

Diagnostic Assessment

Diagnostic assessment identifies characteristics, strengths, weaknesses, knowledge, skills, abilities and any learning difficulties or problems in a new or potential learner with the aim of providing initial advice and guidance both for the learner and the teacher about a particular course of study.

The concept and practice of diagnostic assessment applies to a wide range of assessment activity and can be carried out for a number of purposes. The application of admissions criteria to entrants for a particular course of study that pre-selects potential learners according to prior achievement entails a diagnostic assessment (Tummons, 2011). An example of this would be a sixth form school or college requiring five or more C grades at GCSE for post-16 entry. It is common practice for Year 7 pupils entering secondary school to be given diagnostic assessments in mathematics and English because Key Stage 2 test results are not considered reliable. A learning needs analysis of potential or actual students designed or administered by educationalists is a diagnostic assessment – for example, ICT skills, numeracy, essay writing, oral and written ability in a language. Finally, there is Educational Psychometric Measurement (EPM) such as cognitive diagnostic assessment carried out by specialist educational psychologists. An example would be the Attribute Hierarchy

diagnostic assessment

43

Method (AHM) that generates a skills profile from individuals' responses to tests such as verbal or numerical reasoning.

In most cultures, an educational psychology specialist using psychometric assessments is likely to intervene only in special cases of extreme non-normative performance or behaviour. As a general rule, psychometric tests aim to measure where an individual is located 'on an underlying variable of interest such as science achievement or special aptitude' (Leighton and Gierl, 2007: 10). However, the theoretical foundations upon which these tests are designed have been criticised on various grounds. These include disagreement about theories of cognition and knowledge upon which the conceptualisation of individual items and the range of items in these tests have been based. Technical accuracy in relation to the **validity** and **reliability** of psychometric test design and presuppositions about the theoretical constructs upon which they are based must therefore impose limitations on inferences drawn from the results of such tests. Once these results are communicated from specialist to non-specialist, or from the person undertaking the assessment to the teacher in the classroom, the risk of misinterpretation and inappropriate response inevitably increases.

Concerns associated with diagnostic testing are similar to those around psychometrics in general and cluster around issues of labelling and the effect this has on equality of opportunity, widening participation or positive discrimination, themselves contentious concepts. This can be the case even where the intent behind any diagnostic intervention is to identify the resources required to create a level playing field for the learner in question. The very identification of a learner as someone requiring specialist diagnosis can affect his or her self-concept and attract harm through the behaviours of others towards him or her in (often negative) response to that label. That negative response can apply to a label implying extreme ability, such as gifted and talented, as much as indicating significant learning impairment. The Equality Act 2010 in England and Wales provides a framework for positive action and the allocation of appropriate resources for learners whose needs have been formally identified in this type of diagnostic assessment process.

FURTHER READING

Leighton, J. P. and Gierl, M. J. (2007). *Cognitive Diagnostic Assessment for Education: Theory and Applications*. Cambridge: Cambridge University Press.

Tummons, J. (2011). *Assessing Learning in the Lifelong Learning Sector*. Exeter: Learning Matters.

Differentiation

Differentiation involves designing assessments that are accessible to students of a range of ability, and which also provide stretch and challenge for the highest achieving students.

THE DIFFERENTIATION PROCESS

In the days when progression through the education system was widely regarded as a series of obstacles, over which only a small minority of the population could be expected to jump, differentiation did not need to concern educators or assessors unduly. Now that we have education systems that aspire to cater for the vast majority of the population, assessments have to be conceptualised not as obstacles that signal the point where students will 'drop out' of education, never to return, but as enabling platforms for the next progressive steps in a career of life-long learning. Differentiation is related to, but distinct from **discrimination** (in the sense that this word is used by assessors). The former involves developing challenging and engaging assessments that are meaningful for students of all abilities; the latter involves developing assessment items and tasks that distinguish between students of high, average and low ability.

Differentiation in teaching and assessment can be achieved in various ways, and the educational and social merits of alternative methods of organising schools, colleges and the classes within them, are hotly contested; mixed ability, selection, streaming, banding and setting are just some of the models available. Creating assessments from which teachers can make valid inferences that cater to all ability ranges is challenging.

DIFFERENTIATION IN ASSESSMENT

Differentiation is achieved in two ways: differentiation by task and differentiation by outcome. The GCSE (General Certificate of

differentiation

45

Secondary Education) examination in the UK system is a case in point. There is a clue in the name: the word 'general' signifies that this examination is intended to cater for the vast majority of 14- to 16-year-olds in the UK (there is also a market for adult 'returners' to education).

In certain examination papers in the GCSE system, there is a stress on differentiation by task. In mathematics, for example, it is considered appropriate to use 'tiered' papers, which involve less complex items on the foundation (lower) tier and more complex ones on the higher tier. The highest grades are only available to students capable of coping with more complex tasks. Differentiation by task is more straightforward when there is only one right answer.

Differentiation by outcome is used when questions are more open-ended and how well a student does relies on the standard of his or her response to them, generally assessed through a level of response **mark scheme**. Essays in a history paper are a good example of this sort of differentiation – all students may be asked the same question, such as 'What were the causes of the First World War?', and it is the level of sophistication of their answers that determines how high or low a mark they get.

Where all students sit the same paper the skills of the question setters are put to the test by the extent to which they can set questions designed along an 'incline of difficulty', a mixed-ability target population can work through the paper and each find his or her own best level of challenge and achievement. Typically, the paper will start with more accessible **selection** type questions, for example multiple choice or true and false. Some questions will be scaffolded, that is, divided into parts where the first parts are less challenging and require shorter answers than the following parts. Towards the end of the paper, questions will become more open-ended, with discursive answers being expected, such as essay questions, which require analysis and evaluation.

Within each kind of assessment, it is, of course, possible to identify elements of differentiation by both task and outcome.

FURTHER READING

Chapman, C. and King, R. (2005). *Differentiated Assessment Strategies: One Tool Doesn't Fit All*. Thousand Oaks, CA: Corwin Press.

Miller, D., Linn, R. L. and Gronlund, N. E. (2009). *Measurement and Assessment in Teaching*. (10th edn). Upper Saddle River, NJ: Pearson Education.

Discrimination

> Discrimination is a measure of an assessment's effectiveness in separating high-achieving students from those who achieve less.

Discrimination is related to but distinct from **differentiation**. Discrimination, when used in educational assessment, is not related to the everyday use of the term, that is, to act unfairly to someone because of his or her ethnicity, social class, disability or gender (see **fairness**). Ideally, assessments should not inadvertently rest upon cultural, social or linguistic assumptions that act to disadvantage any individuals or groups of learners. Instead, discrimination as understood by assessors is a positive way to measure how effectively test items and tasks behave in ensuring that so-called 'high achievers' can do well and 'lower achievers' do less well on assessment instruments.

BUILDING DISCRIMINATION INTO AN ASSESSMENT

Imagine a mathematics assessment for 11-year-olds. It is a simple task to construct an assessment that is so easy that everyone who tries it can score 100%. It is also an easy exercise to construct an assessment that is so difficult that everyone scores zero marks. For example, if the test only contained items that called for the addition of single digit numbers then almost every test taker would get the entire test correct and the teacher would not be able to ascertain who was stronger mathematically. Conversely, if all of the items relied on algebra to answer correctly almost no one would be able to answer. Neither test contains items that discriminate effectively among test takers. Ideally, assessments should contain numerous items that 50% of test takers will get correct and 50% will get wrong. These items are the most effective discriminators. In order to ensure that assessments can still be positive experiences for low achievers and can stretch and challenge the most able, items that are less effective discriminators must be included. Experienced, skilled assessors can construct assessments that result in a spectrum of marks, and these marks, and therefore the reported grades, are achieved not through guesswork or good luck but by actual achievement on the part of students.

MEASURING DISCRIMINATION

Statistical techniques can be used to measure the discrimination of a whole assessment. Assessments that produce a normal bell-curve distribution of scores are usually assumed to be discriminating well. Statistics can also measure the discrimination of individual items within an assessment. In a multiple-choice test, for example, individual items can be analysed to see whether students who do well on the individual item also do well on the test as a whole. This can be done by a 'point biserial correlation' between the scores on the item and the scores on the test as a whole. Alternatively, a measure can be arrived at from the proportion of the top third of candidates (as measured by the test as a whole) responding correctly *minus* the proportion of the bottom third responding correctly. A low discrimination (for example, below about 0.20 for point biserial correlations) indicates either that the item is a poor test element, perhaps because it encourages guessing, or that although the item might be a good assessment of whatever trait it measures, that trait is different from the one measured by the test as a whole.

FURTHER READING

Miller, D., Linn, R. L. and Gronlund, N. E. (2009). *Measurement and Assessment in Teaching* (10th edn). Upper Saddle River, NJ: Pearson Education.
Odendahl, N. V. (2011). *Testwise: Understanding Educational Assessment*. Plymouth: Rowman & Littlefield Education.

key concepts in
educational assessment

48

 E-Assessment

This involves assessment tasks, systems and/ or processes designed, accessed and stored through the medium of information and communication technology.

The term e-assessment is a consequence of the information and communications technology (ICT) revolution in education and society in general. It is a reflection of the impact that educational and learning technologies have had upon the education system, including the need to rethink approaches to curriculum and assessment policy. Laurillard anticipated this impact in 1993, stating that 'new technology changes both the curriculum and the way content is known. If assessment is to match what students have learned, it is likely that assessment requirements and standards will change' (1993: 247).

Nicol (2007b) argues that 'there is a growing interest in the use of computers to streamline the delivery of formative assessment tests and of teacher feedback' (p. 670). He also states (2007a) that e-assessment in the form of computer-assisted assessment (CAA) will bring the pedagogical benefits of linking online assessment to sophisticated forms of student **feedback**, in which the technology supports innovative models of formative assessment. Computer adaptive testing (CAT) is a sophisticated example of technology-assisted assessment (Gershon, 2005) in which a computer-based on-screen assessment is designed so that it intelligently adapts to the student's ability after each feedback question cycle. Boyle and Hutchison (2009: 311) debate the merits and limitations of sophisticated tasks in e-assessment using 'media rich stimulus material (graphical, sound, video or animation)' with which the test taker must interact in a variety of ways. They acknowledge that these more complex tasks enable more profound assessments of individuals to be made but also that they present new and unexpected challenges.

E-assessment is a flexible term that relates to a variety of technology-assisted assessment activities ranging from on-screen marking and reporting by assessors to students being assessed on-screen and potentially online. The UK-based Joint Information Systems Committee (JISC) describes on-screen marking and reporting as 'covering a range of activities in which digital technologies are used in ... marking – by computers, or humans assisted by scanners and online tools – and all processes of reporting, storing and transferring of data associated with public and internal assessments' (JISC, 2007: 8). The main GCSE and A level **awarding bodies** widely use on-screen marking.

JISC distinguishes e-assessment systems from computer-based assessment (CBA), which is seen as an interface from which assessment is delivered and marked by the computer, e.g. on-screen or online multiple-choice questions. It provides the following overall definition of e-assessment as 'end-to-end electronic assessment processes where ICT is used for the presentation of assessment activity, and the recording of responses. This includes the end-to-end assessment process from the perspective of learners, tutors, learning establishments, awarding bodies and regulators, and the general public' (JISC, 2007: 6).

Ripley (2006) considers e-assessment as progressing through four main evolutionary phases that can be further adapted and understood in terms of wider educational assessment development:

1 The personalisation of technology that drives **assessment for learning** opportunities.
2 Tests and assessment that will be transformed to include simulations related to problem solving virtual learning environments, i.e. testing higher-order thinking and transferable skills.
3 The migration of paper-based tests to on-screen solutions that go beyond the traditional MCQ platform, which is often regarded as unsophisticated.
4 The development of e-portfolios as an online formative assessment resource. An e-portfolio can be linked to **self-assessment**, **coursework** and **work-based assessment** tasks. This also relates to supporting skills-based projects located within **vocational assessment** curricula.

In the USA, educational technology-enhanced assessment systems are related to the field of instructional technology or the emerging field of instructional design and technology, which combines curriculum development with technology-based assessment systems (Roblyer and Edwards, 2000). In the UK and Europe, there is now a professional body representing e-assessment called the eAssessment Association (eAA).

Integrating technology into teaching and learning can be seen as an educational opportunity through which advanced e-assessment systems (Crisp, 2007; Laurillard, 1993) can be developed such as online e-portfolios (Coombs, 2010) to support formative and self-regulated learning activities (Nicol, 2007b). Online reflective thinking, operating as part of an e-learning environment, can capture qualitative evidence as part of self-assessment learning tasks. Where learning technologies can support ongoing curriculum coursework with intelligent online feedback systems, it can be argued that technology brings an ideal form of assessment for learning, an agenda promoted by Futurelab (2007).

In 1998 Randy Bennett of ETS predicted a three-generation model for adopting e-assessment:

1 Assessments that automate an existing process without reconceptualising it (assessments look like paper-based cousins).
2 Assessments that incorporate advances in technology, psychometrics and cognitive science (audio, video, animation; re-engineered scoring techniques; questions created based on theories of item difficulty drawn from cognitive psychology; all facets done over the internet).
3 Tests that are a radical departure, with distance learning assessment completely embedded in electronic curricula (virtual reality simulations that model complex environments). (Bennett, 1998)

Should his predictions have come to fruition by now? It could be argued that mainstream assessment systems mostly are still stuck in the first generation and have made tentative steps into the second. Given the learning benefits technology can purportedly bring to educational assessment, it is interesting to wonder why Ken Boston's (2005) prophecy of most UK public examinations becoming on-screen by 2010 has not materialised. The answer possibly lies in unanswered questions surrounding the issues of plagiarism, comparability of assessments across the technology divide, and equal access for all learners to technology. Educators, awarding bodies and governments are averse to taking risks in a high-stakes assessment environment, coupled with the practical difficulties of setting up assessments so that all assessment takers can simultaneously access the technology. E-assessment is also expensive to implement initially.

The Apprenticeship, Skills, Children and Learning Act of 2009 stated that the Office of Qualifications and Examinations Regulation (Ofqual) should be encouraging innovation in qualifications and to that end Ofqual has been cautiously promoting e-assessment, most recently through an e-assessment toolkit for practitioners and awarding bodies (see http://toolkit.efutures.org/).

FURTHER READING

Futurelab (2007). *E-assessment – an update on research, policy and practice. Report 10.* Available at: http://archive.futurelab.org.uk/resources/documents/lit_reviews/Assessment_Review_update.pdf

JISC (2010) *Effective assessment in a digital age.* Available at: http://www.jisc.ac.uk/publications/programmerelated/2010/digiassess.aspx

> An examination or test is an attempt to measure a learner's knowledge, understanding or skill within a certain subject or sector domain in a limited amount of time.

PURPOSE

Before we can determine whether an examination fulfils its purpose, we need to understand what that purpose is. Gordon Stobart (2008) lists a number of purposes that any examination may seek to achieve:

- selection and certification
- determining and raising standards
- formative assessment – assessment *for* learning.

Stobart (2008) suggests that there are individual, professional and managerial purposes as well as those listed above. These purposes often overlap and sometimes compete. For example, success in an examination may be used to determine the type of university course that an individual may wish to pursue. Here the examination has selection and certification purposes for the individual and is high stakes because it has important consequences.

However, institutions are also held to account for their success in high-stakes examinations. In such instances, the managerial purposes of assessment have come to dominate individual and professional purposes, even though the initial intention of the examination was to certificate and accredit individuals. Stobart terms this 'managerial creep' – the interaction and competing aims between the different purposes of the same examination.

UNINTENDED CONSEQUENCES

Where an examination's purpose is to certificate an individual's skills and understanding, we need to consider the consequences of what is meant by ability. In *Testing Testing: Social Consequences of the Examined Life*, Hanson (1994: 68) argues that 'the individual in contemporary society is not so much described by tests as constructed by them'.

Hanson (1994) infers that high-stakes tests have become so important that examination success or lack of it 'constructs' the individual rather than 'reflects' what he or she knows, understands and can do. Further, it does this in a way that reflects what society deems important rather than the inherent abilities of the individual in a particular domain. In other words, assessment and examinations are a social construct.

The examination system determines which subjects are important and has an impact upon teaching and the ways in which schools and colleges organise their curricula. These are just some of the unintended consequences of high-stakes assessment.

FORMAL TESTING

A formal examination will result in a score or a mark, which can be interpreted in one of two ways. They can be **norm referenced** or **criterion referenced**; occasionally they can be interpreted by using both methods. Norm referencing depends upon statistical analysis and grades are awarded dependent upon the rest of the cohort's scores and where on a normal distribution curve the individual's score falls. Criterion referencing means an individual's grade depends upon the degree to which his or her answer fulfils set criteria.

STANDARDISATION

All formal and high-stakes examinations and tests are standardised, that is they are administered, fixed in their scope and level of difficulty and marked in a consistent way. This allows the examination a measure of transparency and the outcomes of the examination can be scrutinised to ensure **reliability, validity, fairness** and equity.

Many countries require learners to take standardised tests at some point in their educational career. The timings of these tests differ, as do their administrative procedures. However, to gain access to higher education it is usual for individuals to take leaving or exit examinations. Many professions also use standardised examinations to secure access to the profession.

A number of countries use standardised test scores to judge the performance of individual institutions and hold them to account. In England, this function is carried out by Ofsted, which categorises schools according to known criteria: poor, requires improvement, good and outstanding. In this way, individual institutions are held to account by the performance of their learners in high-stakes assessments.

ADVANTAGES AND DISADVANTAGES

There are a number of advantages of these types of examinations. Because test administrators take pains to ensure accessibility for all, the tests can be seen as both fair and an efficient way of determining an individual's knowledge, skills and understanding. They are deemed efficient because the end user exerts only a limited amount of effort in analysing and interpreting the results. However, the over-reliance on test scores can also be seen as limiting to the curriculum and encouraging teaching to the test. Learners, rather than securing mastery of a particular domain, merely learn to pass the examination.

Nevertheless, the tests' outcomes allow teachers and learners to adapt teaching and learning according to the **feedback** given by such examinations. Over the past 30 years in the summative examinations held in England, Wales and Northern Ireland, there has been a year-on-year improvement in performance, leading experts such as Robert Coe to question the rigour of the assessment process and to question whether examinations are fit for purpose (Coe, 2010). This has brought into doubt the rigour of the predictive qualities claimed for such tests.

By using the outcomes of examinations as accountability measures, high-stakes tests provide an opportunity to hold teachers, lecturers and tutors to account – the managerial purposes of examinations. Despite the fact that individual examinations may have been designed to certificate or accredit individuals, this managerial purpose becomes the overriding factor. Research has been carried out on this phenomenon, particularly in the USA. Many reports submitted to the State Higher Education Executive Officers (SHEEO) conclude that although there can be some positive effects of test-driven accountability measures, the numbers of variables involved makes comparisons difficult and any conclusions less than reliable (SHEEO, 2003).

Coe, R. (2010). 'Understanding comparability of examination standards'. *Research Papers in Education*, 25 (3), 271–84.

Newton, P., Baird, J. A., Goldstein, H., Patrick, H. and Tymms, P. (eds) (2007). *Techniques for Monitoring the Comparability of Examination Standards*. London: QCA.

Valijarvi, J. (2008). *Changing Assessment Practices. Keynote speech*. Available at: www.ciea.co.uk

External Verification

> External verification is a quality assurance mechanism operated by an awarding organisation that ensures that assessment processes carried out by centres have been done correctly, fairly and to the appropriate standard. It confirms or moderates internal school, college or training provider verification processes.

External verification is a means of **quality assuring** locally run and internally marked or graded assessments such as vocational **coursework** assignments, through making judgements about the standard of the provider's internal assessment systems and processes. This usually involves using external verifiers as qualified assessors or examiners to carry out this fieldwork task.

In the university sector, this generally involves a verification system in which external examiners are appointed to ensure **fairness** and equity of internal assessment procedures with independent feedback reports sent to the university as part of overall quality assurance (QA). In the UK, this QA system for higher education is governed by the Quality Assurance Agency (QAA).

external verification

55

Outside of universities, **awarding bodies** provide their own system of external verification to schools, colleges, training providers and workplaces licensed to administer their qualifications and systems of assessment. An external verifier works in partnership with centre-appointed internal verifiers who coordinate the **internal verification** assessment process on behalf of the awarding body (Gravells, 2010). External verifiers are qualified assessors who oversee the assessment process of centres through directly scrutinising the local assessment methods employed against the awarding body's specified criteria. This role helps awarding bodies to achieve equity of internal assessment results across all centres through an approved policy of fairness, objectivity and **validity**, and this process is usually maintained through a common system of **moderation** that applies mainly to vocational and occupational qualifications and is overseen in the UK by the Office of Qualifications and Examinations Regulation (Ofqual).

Taking into account candidate numbers as well as centre assessor and internal verifier numbers, external verifiers visit providers in order to confirm that appropriately qualified staff carry out assessments. They sample centres' assessment decisions to confirm that they are valid and of the appropriate standard. They also advise and support centres on the interpretation of standards and on awarding body procedures, including fair access arrangements.

Sampling is carried out in a way that, over time, covers the assessment decisions of all internal verifiers and assessors, all assessment methods, all assessment locations and candidates at different stages of their qualification. Formal reports provide feedback to centres, including areas of good practice and any measures a centre must take to rectify quality issues (QCA, 2006b).

International awarding bodies such as the International Baccalaureate Organisation (IBO) absorb the role of external verifier into their overall examiner function and policy towards moderation and specify that examiners are appointed to mark externally assessed work or to moderate internally assessed components (reviewing the original marking of teachers).

John Konrad (2000) criticised the assessment and verification framework for delivering the UK's National Vocational Qualifications (NVQs), which he described as being based too much upon a quality control system. He argued that **vocational assessment** policy should shift away from evidence of de-contextualised task compliance and competence to more authentic situated learning activities through quality framework teams, in which the roles of internal and external verifiers and other local assessors were linked in a shared understanding of the social practices and activities involved around more authentic forms of assessment. One good example of a professional learning community of practice is the network of Chartered Educational Assessors who are being trained and licensed by the Chartered Institute of Educational Assessors (CIEA).

FURTHER READING

International Baccalaureate Organisation (IBO). (n.d.). *IB diploma programme examining roles*. Available at: http://www.ibo.org/examiners/assistant_posts/index.cfm
Chartered Institute of Educational Assessors (CIEA). Available at: http://www.ciea.co.uk

USEFUL WEBSITES

Office of Qualifications and Examinations Regulation (Ofqual). Available at: http://www.ofqual.gov.uk
Quality Assurance Agency (QAA). Available at: http://www.qaa.ac.uk/pages/default.aspx

Fairness

> For an assessment to be fair, the content, its context and the expectation of the assessment's performance should provide all candidates with an equal opportunity to demonstrate their ability.

The concept of fairness in assessment and any **examinations** system derives from two key principles: the first is that any assessment system itself is not subject to any form of bias relative to its candidates; and the second is that there is equity of access to whatever system and mode of assessment is on offer.

Historically, one of the original modes of assessment concentrated on a system of **oral assessment** that could be subject to social bias (e.g. gender, ethnicity, religion, social class) through personal knowledge between the examiner and the candidate. This system was largely superseded after the 18th century at Oxford and Cambridge by written examinations (Stray, 2001) that could be more rigorously applied through the design of common questions and assessed through a system of 'blind' marking. Anonymised, written examinations were perceived to be more 'fair' and independent of a candidate's social circumstances.

Fairness requires us to consider an individual candidate's needs and then to make reasonable adjustments to arrangements to ensure equity of access.

Any assessment system adhering to a policy of fair access to its regime of assessment needs to ensure social equity through appropriate design of its methodology and practice (Ofqual, 2010). This implies that candidates should not be disadvantaged because of gender, socio-economic background, ethnic, cultural or religious background, any physical or sensory impairment, any difficulties they face in processing language or any emotional or behavioural problems from which they may suffer (QCA, 2006a). To implement such a policy, the assessment must also be flexible, allowing the individual to display the knowledge, understanding or skill being assessed in a range of circumstances, using whichever assessment methodology is appropriate for the context. This also requires clear communication between assessor and candidate, so that the candidate can access the assessment process whatever the circumstances.

To ensure such equality of access, the language used in the assessment or in examination questions, usually called *carrier language* (Chartered Institute of Educational Assessors, 2007), needs to be accessible to all individuals taking that level of assessment or examination. Although a worthy aspiration, this requirement implies common agreement about cultural competence, including the belief that there is such a 'language in common' between all involved in the assessment process. In practice, this may prove impossible to regulate.

In many standardised examinations, an individual may apply for arrangements to enable access to the examination question. For example, someone with a visual impairment may ask for the text of the question paper to be enlarged or delivered in Braille. Such terms and conditions are often subsumed under a framework of 'reasonable adjustments' to satisfy the disability and discrimination laws of the country in which the assessment takes place. Offering access via online assessment brings its own benefits, challenges and limitations. Although recent technological developments have helped in the design of **e-assessment** platforms, such assessments are still not accessible to all. It is now common in many western democracies for learners to be taught using a variety of technological devices, which are then abandoned for a summative examination, which relies heavily on paper and pen.

Conversely, **e-assessment** systems need to ensure that the technical demands of undertaking an assessment online, such as the ICT skills required of the candidate, do not detract from the **validity** of the content of the assessment because they require the use of skills, which do not form part of the subject being assessed. These have to be balanced against the integrity of the assessment, ensuring that the assessment remains valid. For example, a candidate may be disadvantaged in a science test because the level of language used in the test is at a higher level than the science being assessed. Such events are known technically as construct irrelevance variations, that is to say, the assessment is measuring more than it intends to do – in this case language as well as science – and is therefore unfair to the candidate. Conversely, what if an assessment of language skills at EQF level 3 (European Union, 2008) is presented using language more appropriate to a level 2 qualification? Here is a case of construct under-representation where the assessment fails to measure things that it should. In both cases there are threats to the validity of the assessment.

As well as balancing the issues relating to accessibility and validity, we must also consider the issues relating to bias in relation to groups or sub-groups of candidates such as gender, disability, ethnicity and religion. Fairness and accessibility relate to individual candidates involved in an assessment, whereas bias, relates to groups of candidates rather than individuals. To avoid bias an assessment must use contexts that reflect the experiences of all groups of candidates in what can be seen as a balanced way by all candidates. The language used within the assessment must not disparage any sub-groups within society nor portray narrow and stereotypical representations of sections of society, and the contexts used within the assessment must be familiar to all groups or sub groups within the cohort involved in the assessment.

In addition to issues in the design of and access to assessment, assessors need to ensure fairness in the marking and scoring of assessments. This raises two types of concern. The first relates to how the assessment task is presented to candidates. The second relates to **reliability**, in how the marking and scoring process is carried out by the team of assessors.

fairness

A fair presentation of the assessed task means ensuring that the assessment criteria are clearly stated; that the candidates understand how much each question is worth, how much time to spend on it and how to show the assessor how much they know; and finally, that the candidates understand the nature of the task required and can engage with it in a flexible way. Ensuring fairness in the design and administration of the assessment task leads to the achievement of equity in the assessment process.

Lack of equity is a challenge to the validity of an assessment. This is particularly important in public systems of high-stakes educational assessment that need to be socially inclusive (Gipps and Stobart, 2009). In Australasia, the Australasian Curriculum, Assessment and Certification Authorities (2011) enshrine in law the need to ensure equity even at item level. Similarly, in South Africa, the South African Qualifications Authority (SAQA) has published *Criteria and Guidelines for Assessment of National Qualification Framework (NQF) Registered Unit Standards and Qualifications*, where accessibility arrangements are clearly outlined and this has also been updated as a key policy statement regarding the efficacy and efficiency of the NQF (South African Qualifications Authority, 2007).

Following the implementation of any assessment, it is important to monitor its outputs and check that it has performed in an unbiased and equitable way. This is achieved by analysis of the data emanating from different assessed groups to check if there is a similar distribution of results for different groups of similar abilities. Thus, we can check the data for its impact upon, for instance, gender or ethnicity – do the different genders or ethnic groups perform in the same way for the assessment as a whole and for individual items within the assessment?

Such monitoring and evaluation of results is important to ensure overall equity in the implementation of any assessment system. For example, in a recent contribution to the field of equity and assessment, and in order to gain insight into teacher expectations, Strand looked at tiering, generally considered to be a sound assessment strategy. Amongst other things, he found Black Caribbean pupils to be under-represented in entry to higher tiers, even after controlling for prior attainment and a wide range of other factors (Strand, 2010).

If an assessment is to be fair and equitable, it must give fair access to those individuals engaging with the assessment, as well as be unbiased towards different sub-groups within the cohort.

FURTHER READING

Gipps, C. and Stobart, G. (2009). 'Fairness in assessment'. In C. Wyatt-Smith and J. Cumming (eds), *Educational Assessment in the 21st Century* (pp. 105–18). London: Springer.

Qualifications and Curriculum Authority (QCA) (2006a). *Fairness by Design*. London: QCA.

Feedback

Feedback is a process through which students learn how well they are achieving and what they need to do to improve their performance. Successful feedback should be two-way, with learners acting upon the feedback they are given.

One way of conceptualising feedback in education is to view it as a stimulus that elicits a response, such as constructive comment on the strengths and weaknesses of a student's work on an assessment task. Feedback achieves its purpose only if it brings about a modification in the student's future learning behaviour and/or the teacher's teaching content or style. In nature, feedback is always a two-way process, something which is often forgotten in man-made systems such as educational assessment, where participants occupying positions in the upper levels of a hierarchy sometimes view feedback as a top-down process without a corresponding flow of information in the other direction.

SYSTEMATIC, TWO-WAY FEEDBACK

The existence of a 'feedback' loop was highlighted by Kolb (1984) in his 'learning cycle' as an essential feature that distinguishes a system from a non-system. Properly organised, feedback provides an automatic self-regulating mechanism that informs teachers and learners and

feedback

prepares them for the next cycle in the learning process. Similarly, Dylan Wiliam (2009) identified two connected feedback systems: students feed back to teachers about what they are doing, what they believe they need to do next, what they need by way of help and tuition. Teachers use the outcomes of student assessments both formative and summative, together with feedback from students, as a guide to the success or otherwise of the student experience, talk to each other about what students are saying, change their practice accordingly, and feed back to students on their progress and on what happens next. This involves students and teachers in a continuous, systematic loop, a policy of continuous improvement. Teachers and students actively cooperate in learning, rather than students being passive recipients of knowledge and skills, and teachers being passive carriers of officially prescribed methods.

Royce Sadler (1989), in writing about Ramaprasad's definition of feedback, highlighted the importance of learners taking on board feedback that they are given – closing the gap between teaching and learning:

> An important feature of Ramaprasad's definition is that information about the gap between actual and reference levels is considered as feedback only when it is used to alter the gap. If the information is simply recorded, passed to a third party who lacks either the knowledge or the power to change the outcome, or is too deeply coded (for example, as a summary grade given by the teacher) to lead to appropriate action, the control loop cannot be closed, and 'dangling data' substituted for effective feedback. (p. 121)

Feedback data cannot simply identify the gap between learners' current and desired performance levels – the data must be used. Wiliam (2011) posits that if feedback is employed just to describe existing levels of performance then its original, robust meaning as a system is lost.

A number of meta-analyses of feedback have pointed to positive effect sizes. Yet, Kluger and DeNisi (1996) warned that many of the possible feedback interventions could have a negative effect on students. For example, students might respond to feedback indicating that their performance exceeded a goal by deciding that the goal was too easy and decreasing their efforts. If told their performance has not met the goal, they might reduce their aspirations or abandon the goal entirely because they think the goal is unreachable.

EFFECTIVE FEEDBACK

The goal of good feedback is essentially the same as that for the final element of formative assessment: 'to decide where the learners are in their learning; where they need to go; and *how best to get there*' (Assessment Reform Group, 2002: 1, emphasis added). Effective feedback will help the learner to 'close the gap' between current knowledge, skills and understanding and his or her learning goals. Hattie and Timperley (2007: 104) in their seminal work on feedback stated that 'to be effective feedback needs to be clear, purposeful, meaningful, and compatible with students' prior knowledge and to provide logical connections'. They found that some forms of feedback, such as cues, corrective feedback, motivational influences and reinforcement had far larger effect sizes than other types, such as teacher praise and rewards and punishments. In their model, effective feedback must answer three questions: 'Where am I going?' 'How am I going?' and 'Where to next?' (Hattie and Timperley, 2007: 87). The first involves an understanding among students and teachers of what the learning goals consist of – sometimes known as success criteria – the second is about the students' understanding of their own progress against performance goals and the last helps learners to know how to move on from the learning they may have already consolidated in order to achieve overall learning goals.

Torrance and Pryor (1998) wrote about a continuum of assessment approaches with 'convergent assessment' at one end of the spectrum and 'divergent assessment' at the other. Convergent assessment feedback – also known as 'directive feedback' (Black and Wiliam, 1998a) and 'task-focused feedback' (Hattie and Timperley, 2007) – is when teachers try to get what are perceived to be the correct answers from students and where they correct students' errors. Divergent assessment feedback – or 'facilitative feedback' (Black and Wiliam, 1998a) or 'process-focused/self-regulation-focused feedback' (Hattie and Timperley, 2007) is more challenging for the student and teacher alike – where feedback is 'exploratory, provisional or provocative' (Pryor and Crossouard, 2008: 4). This type of feedback encourages students to take control of their own ideas.

According to the research, feedback should be clearly linked with the learning intention or criteria, that is, students must be able to understand what they were meant to learn or do and what success on that learning goal would look like. If students do not understand the learning goals then they cannot know how to interpret any feedback they receive. This means sharing success criteria with learners from the outset. Those success criteria can be negotiated with the learners, which can increase their value to the learner. Students should believe themselves to be an important part of the learning environment, in which the feedback that they receive concentrates on the learning itself rather than the learner. Positive, informative feedback encourages students to continue making an effort and improve their subsequent work. However, it is important to avoid what Torrance and Pryor (1998) described as 'criteria compliance' – where ticking off the objectives and criteria take on a greater importance than the learning itself and where feedback is overly directive. Giving grades or marks can sometimes interfere with effective feedback because learners do not look beyond the letter or number to any comments made on their work (Lipnevich and Smith, 2009).

Any feedback should be about the student's work rather than about the student him- or herself. Hattie and Timperley (2007) found that praise ('good girl') was the least effective type of feedback because students could learn nothing from it. This sort of feedback is about the student herself rather than her accomplishments and neglects to provide the necessary information about what the student has done and how she can improve her learning – good learning in this case could seem to be simply that which attracts praise.

According to Hargreaves (2011), good descriptive feedback includes an explanation of how and why the student either achieved against the criteria or still needs to work toward achieving this. For example, in history, feedback might include, 'You have successfully described the alliances that formed before the First World War. Your challenge now is to explain the effect of those alliances in causing the outbreak of war'. The students will need to be given clues about the appropriate standards for their next steps – these should be stretching, but achievable in order to avoid frustration. It should be up to the learner to reflect on his or her learning and derive next steps from the feedback provided. The claim is that productive feedback will encourage the student to change positively his or her approach to future learning.

Feedback should be effectively timed so that learners are able to make best use of it and it should be as understandable as possible and in small enough pieces so that students are not overwhelmed and do not therefore discard it. According to Mayer and Moreno (2002), presenting too much information may not only result in superficial learning but may also invoke cognitive overload, where students who receive too much information or are asked to do too much cannot process this information and become anxious or feel stressed. If feedback is given during the activity or task, it means that students can use it while the task is still fresh in their minds. There should be an appropriate balance between immediate or delayed, written or oral responses that suits the purpose of the feedback.

Effective feedback focuses on how students are assessing and reflecting on their own and others' learning, collaborating with others in learning, transforming information they get in order to understand and remember the material, motivating themselves to complete work, persevering in the face of failure and contributing in class (Stobart, 2011).

Students can engage in self and peer feedback (also known as **self-assessment** and **peer-assessment**). Self-assessment involves students thinking about what and how they are learning during the process of learning – this is a form of internal feedback that helps them ascertain whether they need to adjust their learning strategies (Heritage, 2010). Feedback from peers benefits both the person receiving the feedback and the person giving it. Done in a constructive way, it calls upon students to have dialogues with peers about mutual learning goals and helps deepen both parties' understanding of those goals.

Eleanor Hargreaves (2011) writes about provocative feedback, which she theorises is useful in helping students think more critically about their learning. Provocative feedback aims to get the learner to think deeply, question him- or herself, have new ideas, reflect on the learning and take action. According to Hargreaves, provocative feedback, by asking students to develop their own way forward and own their learning, reinforces lifelong understanding through provoking sustained changes in thinking, self-reflection and active control over learning. It encourages students to self-regulate by discovering for themselves where learning has been successful and to share good strategies with their peers.

FURTHER READING

Hargreaves, E. (2005). 'Assessment for learning? Thinking outside the (black) box'. *Cambridge Journal of Education*, 35(2), 213–24.

Kluger, A. N. and DeNisi, A. (1996). 'The effects of feedback interventions on performance: a historical review, a meta-analysis, and a preliminary feedback intervention theory'. *Psychological Bulletin*, 119 (2), 254–84.

Mory, E. H. (2004). 'Feedback research review'. In D. H. Jonassen (ed.), *Handbook of Research on Educational Communications and Technology*. Mahwah, NJ: Lawrence Erlbaum (pp. 745–83).

Shute, V. J. (2008). 'Focus on formative feedback'. *Review of Educational Research*, 78 (1), 153–89.

Wiliam, D. (2011) *Embedded Formative Assessment*. London: Solution Tree Press.

feedback

Grading, Including Marking

> Marking is the process of using numbers to signify student achievement. Grading is the process of making an overall judgement of the quality of the work, sometimes through aggregating marks.

Grading and marking serve a variety of purposes – among other things, grades tell students, parents, schools and other interested parties how well students are doing (and sometimes how well the system as a whole is doing); can give students feedback so that they can evaluate their own performance (although those who champion **assessment for learning** are dubious about this aspect); and can be used for selection purposes for progression, such as appropriate further and higher education (Guskey, 2011). So ensuring that the marking and grading processes are as rigorous and fair as possible is extremely important.

This entry uses the definitions of grades and marks found in Sadler (2005): marking refers to the process of using numbers to signify student achievement; grading refers to the process of aggregating marks (and sometimes other information) into an overall judgement of a qualification, a major piece of work or programme of study. Grades are found in letter form (A, B, C, etc.), as descriptors (Distinction, Merit, Pass) or numbers (1st, 2.1, 2.2 in British university outcomes and national curriculum levels 1 to 7 in England; grade point averages [GPA] 0 to 4 in the USA); and/or percentages.

The grading process usually involves using more specific evidence such as the outcomes of **examination** papers, **coursework**, homework, quizzes, etc. to derive more general information, which means that information can be lost and categories of achievement can be quite broad. This – and the inevitable measurement error that accompanies any marking or grading process – leaves open the possibility that students could receive a different grade/level than they deserve. Dylan Wiliam famously put the percentage of misclassified students on national curriculum tests in England at 30% (Wiliam, 2001). Although this figure has been disputed (House of Commons Children, Schools and Families Committee, 2008; Newton, 2009; He *et al.*, 2011), it has become fixed in the minds of the press and the public. Some, such as Koretz (2008), advocate reporting out percentages because they afford finer discrimination and lose less information.

Although norm-based grading (commonly known as grading on a curve in the USA) used to be quite common; over the last few decades criterion- or standards-based grading has become increasingly common (see **norm referencing, criterion referencing**). In this latter form, the criteria used to judge performance and the level (or standard) which that performance is expected to reach, are public information. The reasoning behind using criterion-based grading and marking is that students have a right to know at the outset on what they will be judged and how, without any direct comparison to how well or badly other students have done. The aim is to specify clearly what different achievement levels consist of and should reflect the aims and outcomes of the unit, module, syllabus or course.

Recently, Sadler (2009) has warned against the overly prescriptive use of criteria to generate grades in higher education, pointing out that work that a grader considers brilliant may not be excellent on each and every criterion, and work that is judged mediocre overall can hit all of the right criteria buttons. Instead, he advocates a more holistic approach to generating grades. Outside HE, however, holistic approaches are rarely used.

FROM DEVELOPMENT TO RESULTS

In England, Wales and Northern Ireland, the process of setting standards and deriving grades for national curriculum tests and examinations is enshrined in regulatory codes of practice (see **regulation**). For external examinations, chief and senior examiners prepare draft papers and mark schemes that are reviewed by additional senior examiners and **awarding body** staff and if necessary amended. Once students have sat the examinations, all scripts are returned to the awarding body. Sample scripts are used to revise the **mark scheme**, if necessary; this ensures that students will get credit for right answers that may not have been originally included in the mark scheme. All markers (examiners) are trained in the application of the mark scheme, sometimes in face-to-face meetings and sometimes online. This is to ensure that criteria are not interpreted differently by different markers. As the scripts are being marked, largely online, senior examiners keep the marking under constant review to ensure that markers are being fair and consistent, and not using slightly different standards when tired or bored. If anyone is found to be out of line with the set standards, his or her marking may not be counted and the scripts may be sent to other markers.

Once the **awarding body** has all of the marked scripts, there is a pre-award meeting during which the chair of examiners and awarding body staff identify where problems of consistency and comparability might arise. They look at the ability of those who took the examination, based on past performance, and at the demand of the examination (through mean scores, standard deviations, and seeing what outcomes would be if grade boundary marks remained the same as they were last year). They make preliminary grade boundary recommendations using archived scripts from the year before, as well as statistical information on candidate performance, historical performance, cohort ability and teachers' estimated grades. At the awarding meeting, grading standards are set by reviewing candidates' work at certain borderlines (for example, for A levels the awarding committee looks at the A/B and E/U boundaries; the other boundaries are set arithmetically), reviewing scripts against grade descriptions, comparing work against archive scripts and reviewing the statistical evidence. The chair of examiners signs off the proposed grade boundaries and a senior manager reviews them. In order to ensure that decisions are in line with previous years' standards (see **comparability**) and the statistical evidence, the head of standards within the awarding body is responsible for the ultimate signing off of all awarding committee recommendations. After a 'review of awards' group meets, which includes external members and an observer from the regulator, students' results are generated and sent to schools and colleges. Similar processes are used for setting levels for national curriculum tests and for setting boundaries for coursework and controlled assessment.

The system is imperfect; in the summer of 2011, 12 different GCSE and A level examinations contained mistakes that had to be rectified through the marking and grading processes. There is general discontent among primary teachers in England about the marking of Key Stage 2 English writing tests that led to changes to the marking system in 2012 (see **national curriculum assessment**). There have been calls to substitute teachers' summative judgements for external examining from

Wynne Harlen, Dylan Wiliam, Paul Black and Richard Daugherty, among others. It has, however, not been proven that teacher judgement is more reliable than external examinations and the current government in England shows no signs of abandoning the latter.

FURTHER READING

Guskey, T. R. (2011). 'Five obstacles to grading reform'. *Educational Leadership*, 69 (3), 16–21.

Sadler, D. R. (2009). 'Indeterminacy in the use of preset criteria for assessment and grading'. *Assessment & Evaluation in Higher Education*, 34 (2), 159–79.

Group Assessment

> Group assessment refers to assessment of a group product, assignment or task and/or of a group process. Members of the group might be given a mark or grade in common, each member an individual mark or grade, or, in some contexts marks or grades of individual group members might be aggregated.

This entry covers the assessment of a group task or process as opposed to assessment *by* a group, which is dealt with under **peer assessment**, although it is possible for assessment purpose and design to bring these together. Issues of concern in the design and administration of group assessment relate to its **purposes** and must include **validity, reliability** and **fairness**.

There is a variety of group assessment design types. One requires that a group of learners as a whole is given a mark or grade in common, another that each member of the group is given an individual mark, which is then aggregated for the group as a whole and in yet another, each individual is given an individual mark or grade for his or her particular overall contribution to the group. The main objection to the allocation of a mark to the whole group is one of fairness between individual group members. There is understandable concern that there is a risk that it encourages 'freeloading': 'the most important single issue is often the tricky matter of establishing levels of contribution of respective [group] members' (Race *et al.*, 2005: 156). One way of countering this unevenness of contribution is to make the mark or grade awarded to the group an aggregate of individual marks within the group. In addition to fairness, issues of validity and reliability are equally tricky since the composite margins of error culminating in an aggregate mark or grade are likely to reduce confidence in both of these attributes.

The moderation of group work poses particular problems since group composition cannot possibly replicate the same kinds of individuals with the same skills and attributes. These conditions, therefore, do not enable the establishment of **norm-referenced** scoring between groups. In most situations, it is unlikely that there will be a large enough number of groups undergoing assessment at the same moment whose scores can thus be distributed. Yet assessors, accustomed as they are to being shaped by expectations of a normally distributed range of scores, may find it difficult to **discriminate** very accurately and therefore fairly between groups.

It must be argued, as ever, that the purpose of group assessment is of paramount importance to those planning to take this approach, especially in terms of where it lies in the low-to-high stakes hierarchy of **attainment** and **qualifications**. It will be easier to justify and manage in low-stakes contexts and indeed to argue its merits as a formative rather than summative assessment process. However, group projects are also commonly used in summative assessment in some vocationally related qualifications, and indeed in mainstream education, for example drama and theatre studies. In these instances, different individuals in the group are allocated individual marks, not an aggregated or group mark. A significant issue in the planning of group assessment processes is the allocation of group members. Here, the management of group dynamics and the appropriateness of the method to the sub-culture of the context are similar to those covered in peer assessment.

One of the merits of group assessment, although here it implies a peer marking system, is that it reduces the marking burden for staff. A counter to this is that if unfamiliar it might in fact increase teacher and learner anxiety associated with assessment. Another potential benefit of group assessment is the opportunity it affords to assess learners' group working skills as well as the task skills allocated to the group. The assumption is that teams or groups can achieve more than individuals and tackle more complex issues. The value in this clearly relates to many employment and social situations in which working in groups is the only way of achieving certain aims. These include organisational, communication, team, problem-solving, leadership and management skills, all deemed useful as preparation for employment and for life skills more generally. Boud *et al.* (2001) reinforce difficulties encountered due to unfamiliarity with this mode of assessment, but they suggest that these can be mitigated by creating 'opportunities to build group planning and accountability skills' (p. 75).

FURTHER READING

Bloxham, S. and Boyd, P. (2007). *Developing* Effective *Assessment in Higher Education: A Practical Guide.* Maidenhead: McGraw-Hill.

Li, L.K.Y. (2001). 'Some refinements on peer assessment of group projects'. *Assessment & Evaluation in Higher Education*, 26 (1), 5–18.

Intelligence Quotient (IQ)

IQ is a score on a standardised test that ranks individuals' general aptitudes (intelligence) within population norms. Most common IQ tests have a mean of 100 and a standard deviation of 15. Controversy surrounds both the existence of IQ and the factors, such as race, gender, social class and heredity, which might affect it.

There is probably no concept in educational assessment more controversial than Intelligence Quotient, more commonly called IQ. Assessment experts cannot agree whether or not it exists, no less on how to measure it. The debate over IQ encompasses some very sensitive factors – race, gender, social class, heredity – and it is almost impossible to present the topic neutrally.

The origins of IQ testing lie in the late 19th century when Sir Francis Galton theorised about the heritability of genius, stating that intelligence ran in families, not surprisingly including his own.[1] Although he was unsuccessful in developing tests of intelligence, which he believed could be measured through physical attributes, he did introduce the concept of normally distributed mental abilities.

French psychologist Alfred Binet created the first intelligence tests for educational purposes. In trying to establish which students might be in need of special educational assistance, he put together a series of verbal and pictorial scalable tests in 1905. Through these he developed the notion of a child's mental, rather than chronological, age. By comparing the mental and chronological ages, the tester could label the child as below, at or above average, and provide needed support.

These tests were adapted in the USA (Stanford-Binet tests, by Lewis Terman) and the UK (11+ tests, by Sir Cyril Burt) and were widely used with children over the next 60 years, both to assess those who needed special education and those who might be gifted. The Stanford-Binet Intelligence Scale, first published in 1916, characterised intelligence using a single number, called an intelligence quotient (IQ), based on dividing the testee's mental age by his or her chronological age and multiplying the product by 100. So, for example, a 10-year-old child with a mental age of 11 would have an IQ of 110 (11/10 x 100).

Intelligence tests were also designed to be used to separate out unproductive – i.e. those with low IQs – members of society. Terman, in his 1919 introduction to the Stanford-Binet tests, stated: 'It is safe to predict that in the near future intelligence tests will bring tens of thousands of ... high-grade defectives under the surveillance and protection of society. This will ultimately result in the curtailing of the reproduction of feeblemindedness and in the elimination of enormous amounts of crime, pauperism and industrial inefficiency' (quoted in Gould, 1996: 209).

Whereas Binet's tests were carried out one-to-one and took two hours to administer, large-scale quick-to-administer paper and pencil tests were created during the First World War to test and place recruits to the

US Army. These were known as Alpha (verbal) and Beta (non-verbal) tests. Tests similar to these were used widely in the USA and Europe during the first half of the 20th century for selection in education and the military.

Sir Cyril Burt pioneered intelligence testing in schools in England to select students for grammar school education. He argued that aptitude tests were fairer for working-class children because they were less class-biased than essay tests. These tests became known as the 11-plus examinations.

Most of the early intelligence test developers believed that some races, and/or social classes naturally had lower intelligence than others. Later, others argued that intelligence was malleable and that environmental factors played a large role in a person's intelligence. J. R. Flynn, in what subsequently became known as the Flynn Effect, pointed out that IQ scores have been rising by 0.4% every year since records began. He stated that this must be environmental, since the gene pool has not altered (Flynn, 1999). The 'nature versus nurture' debate is still ongoing, but it has not put a stop to IQ testing.

Stephen Jay Gould, in *The Mismeasure of Man* (1996), argued that there were two main fallacies in the (mis)use of IQ tests. The first is what he called 'reification' – the assumption that test scores represent a single, scalable thing that can be called intelligence; the second he labelled 'hereditarianism' – by which he meant that while intellectual capability can be inherited, heritable does not necessarily mean inevitable. He also pointed to the confusion of within-group and between-group heredity: that if heredity explains a certain amount of variation within a group, it must also explain variability between groups. These, he stated, are separate phenomena, so, for example, average height, although clearly heritable, in a prosperous city in a developed country will inevitably be greater than in a very poor city in a developing one (Gould, 1996).

Others have posited the notion of multiple intelligences, the most well known of which is found in Howard Gardner's 1983 work. Gardner (1983) stated that there were eight main intelligences: spatial; linguistic; logical-mathematical; kinaesthetic; musical; interpersonal; intrapersonal; and naturalistic. Gardner's theories have been criticised as being unprovable and not substantiated by neuro-cognitive research. His learning types have also been taken too literally – where feisty, loud boys are labelled kinaesthetic learners and not expected to succeed in life (Stobart, 2008).

The most commonly used modern IQ tests are the Wechsler tests, first developed in 1939 and most lately revised in 2008. Unlike their predecessors, the tests are standardised using large samples of men and women, a number of ethnic groups, people from urban and rural areas, etc. The tests are calibrated to have a mean of 100 and a standard deviation of 15. They do, however, bear a resemblance to the original Binet tests in that they test verbal ability, memorisation, spatial ability and speed.

NOTE

1 Galton also derived the standard deviation as a variance measure as well as regression and correlation coefficients, all of which underpin assessment theory and practice.

FURTHER READING

Herrnstein, R. J. and Murray, C. A. (1994). *The Bell Curve: Intelligence and Class Structure in American Life.* New York: Free Press.

Jensen, A. R. (1998). *The G Factor: The Science of Mental Ability.* Westport, CT: Praeger.

Wechsler, D. (2003). *Wechsler Intelligence Scale for Children.* (4th edn.). San Antonio, TX: Psychological Corporation.

key concepts in educational assessment

74

Internal Verification

Internal verification is a quality assurance mechanism that operates within a school, college, training provider or workplace that ensures that assessment processes have been carried out correctly and fairly. It often complements external verification, which is carried out by an awarding body.

Internal verification usually relates to the **moderation** and **quality assurance** processes of **awarding body** assessments that are held within an education or training environment. This may be in a school, college, training provider or workplace where practical and **continuous assessments** take place. In school-based and college settings, there will be official quality assurance systems for managing and delivering **coursework**, controlled assessments, **performance-based** and **oral assessment** that are linked to the external awarding body's set of regulations. This usually involves a process of internal verification and moderation of the marking and grading of such *in situ* assessments. The people involved are teachers or supervisors operating as the local assessors working with someone in the team appointed as the internal verifier who is accountable to the awarding body.

The Open College Network (OCN) of the East Midlands region of the UK provides a useful rationale and working definition of internal verification: 'a process undertaken by a providing organisation in which assessment practices and decisions are regularly sampled and evaluated and findings are acted upon to ensure consistency and fairness' (OCNEMR, 2011: 1).

The OCNEMR and other international professional bodies maintain that internal verification involves two key processes: verification and **standardisation**. In **work-based assessment** situations, there may be practical work-based learning assignments linked to standard **vocational assessment** learning objectives as part of the wider vocational education and training syllabus. Awarding body external verifiers work closely with the provider organisation's internal verifier as part of the assessment internal moderation process. Ann Gravells (2010), working within the lifelong learning sector, provides a description of the evidence-based assessment process linked to the quality assurance role of the internal verifier: 'Your learners' evidence and your assessment records will be internally verified within your organisation, and externally verified by an awarding body representative. You may also be inspected by representatives from Ofsted or other regulatory bodies. This ensures a system of quality assurance' (p. 21).

The internal verification process generally includes internal verifiers evaluating the assessment instruments used for each unit or qualification and sampling assessment decisions made on each of those units and by every assessor. Samples need to cover the full range of assessment decisions and the number of assessment decisions sampled must be large enough so that inferences can be drawn about the whole cohort taking the assessment.

The internal assessment and validation of student coursework is considered controversial owing to problems of verifying authenticity of the student's work and issues surrounding potential plagiarism (McCabe and Trevino, 1996). This has put increased pressure on awarding bodies to tighten up the quality assurance arrangements underpinning the roles of the internal and external verifier. There is also a body called the Chartered Institute of Educational Assessors (CIEA) that is a professional association with the remit to support all those involved in marking, moderating and assessment in education. For internal verifiers working in schools, colleges and training centres, it offers local assessors the opportunity to train for a licence called the Chartered Educational Assessor (CEA). Professional associations such as the CIEA encourage networks of teachers to moderate their assessment practice through local communities of practice, which become *de facto* internal verification systems.

USEFUL WEBSITES

Chartered Institute of Educational Assessors (CIEA). Available at: http://www.ciea.co.uk
Office of Qualifications and Examinations Regulation (Ofqual). Available at: http://www.ofqual.gov.uk

International Assessment

Most countries' policy makers believe that educational achievement is the key to economic success and therefore the rank ordering of countries based on their students' outcomes on tests such as PISA, TIMSS and PIRLS can have a wide-reaching effect on education policy.

International comparison of student achievement has had an increased impact over the last two decades as countries increasingly compete in global markets. Most countries' political representatives believe that educational achievement is the key to economic success and therefore the rank ordering of countries based on their students' outcomes on tests can have wide-reaching effects on education policy. The most popular tests are:

THE PROGRAMME FOR INTERNATIONAL STUDENT ASSESSMENT (PISA)

The Organisation for Economic Co-operation and Development (OECD) develops PISA, which is taken by 15-year-olds. PISA has carried out assessments every three years since 2000 with more than 70 countries taking part. All of the OECD nations participate alongside other countries: 43 in 2000; 41 in 2003; 58 in 2006; and 74 in 2009 (OECD, 2011).

PISA assesses reading, mathematical and scientific literacies, each round emphasising one of the literacies in particular. The tests stress problem solving and participants' ability to apply knowledge and skills and to analyse, reason and communicate effectively. The tests are averaged to 500 points with a standard deviation of 100, and the OECD rank orders the countries in each literacy domain.

PISA assesses whether students have got the knowledge and skills necessary to participate in society as adults and purports to cover public policy issues such as: 'Are our schools adequately preparing young people for the challenges of adult life?', 'Are some kinds of teaching and schools more effective than others?' and 'Can schools contribute to improving the futures of students from immigrant or disadvantaged backgrounds?' (OECD, 2011).

The tests are a combination of multiple-choice and constructed items that attempt to capture real-life situations. In addition to the tests, PISA conducts a survey of student attributes such as gender, country of origin, socio-economic background and attitude to learning. Information gathered is then correlated with test scores to see whether or not (and how much) these factors might contribute to achievement (OECD, 2011).

TRENDS IN MATHEMATICS AND SCIENCE STUDY (TIMSS)

TIMSS has been assessing fourth and eighth grade students in mathematics and science every four years since 1995; the 2011 series is its fifth. In 2011, 78 countries and regions took part, both from the developed and the developing world. The TIMSS assessments are tied to the curricula of the participating countries and the International Association for the Evaluation of Educational Achievement (IEA) promotes countries' use of results and other data gathered during the assessment process to inform education policy (TIMSS, 2011).

Through its assessment of both the content and cognitive domains and the background data collected from students, teachers and principals on school resources, curriculum and instruction, the IEA claims that participants can:

- access comprehensive and internationally comparable data
- compare results over time
- identify progress from fourth to eighth grades
- look into the effectiveness of teaching and learning
- understand contexts in which students learn best
- address internal policy issues. (Mullis *et al.*, 2009: 16)

The achievement scale average is 500 with a standard deviation of 100 and the tests consist of both multiple-choice and constructed response items.

PROGRESS IN INTERNATIONAL READING LITERACY STUDY (PIRLS)

International assessment of fourth graders' (at least 9.5 years old) reading ability is done through PIRLS, also run by IEA. Its third cycle took place in 2011, in which over 50 countries from the developed and developing world participated. The test is put together in such a way that participating countries can look at trends over time. Students and parents/carers are also asked to fill in a questionnaire about their reading experiences at home, and teacher and principal questionnaires explore experiences in school (PIRLS, 2011).

The assessments concentrate on three aspects of reading literacy: purposes of reading; processes of comprehension; and reading behaviours and attitudes, and contain multiple-choice and constructed response items. The achievement scale average is 500 with a standard deviation of 100. Reading passages are carefully checked for cultural bias, since they must be used across many countries.

USES AND ABUSES OF INTERNATIONAL ASSESSMENT

All three international assessments claim to have educational policy uses and to help participating countries shape and reform their curriculum and governance systems. Although rank orderings are generally reported out with caveats, such as the statistical significance of the difference between scores, such nuance is often lost in public debate. After PISA 2000, there was 'policy shock' in Germany when it fell down the rankings table. Subsequent policy reforms included developing new standards for measuring students' achievement and increased assessment at primary and secondary levels (Grek, 2009). Finland, whose students have recently scored well on international assessments, has been widely visited by representatives from other nations who want to learn from its success.

According to Hopmann and Brinek (2007, quoted in Rutkowski and Rutkowski, 2010: 414), 'every time a new PISA wave rolls in, or an additional analysis appears, governments fear the results, newspapers fill column after column, and the public demands answers to the claimed failings in the country's school system'. The 2007 PIRLS results showed that England had fallen in reading from third to nineteenth, although still significantly about the international mean. The government reacted by stating that parents must do more – blaming TVs, mobile phones and computer games (BBC, 2007). When in 2008 England ranked among the top 10 in the TIMSS assessment of 10- and 14-year-olds, it was time for governmental crowing (BBC, 2008). But it was back to regret and anger when in 2010 the latest round of PISA was reported, with UK schools once again falling in the global ranking. The government now stated that there was an 'urgent need to reform our school system' (BBC, 2010).

Haahr et al. (2005) point out that only approximately one tenth of total variation in student performance lies between countries and the other nine-tenths lie within countries. They claim that countries should pay attention to differences between education systems and programmes, between schools and between students within schools.

FURTHER READING

Grek, S. (2009). 'Governing by numbers: the PISA "effect" in Europe'. *Journal of Education Policy*, 24 (1), 23–37.

Haahr, J. H., Nielsen, T. K., Jakobsen, S. T. and Hansen, M. E. (2005). *Explaining Student Performance: Evidence from the International PISA, TIMSS and PIRLS Surveys*. European Commission, Directorate General for Education and Culture.

Ipsative Assessment

> Ipsative assessment is a mode of assessment in which the assessed individual is compared to him- or herself either in the same field through time or in comparison with other fields. It is used in and sometimes referred to as 'profiling'. In education, ipsative assessment means the assessment is referenced to learners' former performances, resulting in a descriptor expressed in terms of their 'personal best'.

The core purpose of ipsative, or self-referenced, assessment in educational contexts is to measure or track the progress of the individual by comparing his or her performance, or scores, against his or her own previous performances or scores. The 'personal best' performance is denoted as the standard against which the outcome is judged without any reference to the performance of others. It can be contrasted in particular with **norm-referenced** assessment, since it does not compare the individual with peers in a year group or cohort. Although it is generally also contrasted with **criterion-referenced** assessment, specific individually designed criteria may or may not be used depending on what aspect of knowledge, understanding or skill is being assessed. It is typically used in sport, physical education and more recently in online gaming where the concept of 'personal best' has currency.

Ipsative assessment is deemed to improve motivation where the element of competition with others has been removed and for certain types of learners (for example, those with low self-esteem and/or a track record of low attainment). It can be an appropriate approach for learners with learning disabilities since it is, by definition, an individuated approach designed to accommodate the needs and goals of the individual. It is also valued where peer pressure is deemed to produce a demotivating factor.

The locus of control with ipsative assessment might be shared with a teacher or coach, or it might rest entirely with the individual being

key concepts in
educational assessment

80

assessed. In the former case, the teacher and learner will work together to identify particular individual strengths and weaknesses, define the particular goals or targets against which future progress will be assessed and articulate how these will be resourced and met. In the latter case, the individual will take sole responsibility for all aspects of the process. This requires a relatively high degree of understanding of what learning is to be achieved, how it will take place and what barriers may be encountered en route. An ipsative approach to assessment design and implementation can be a powerful tool for enhancing a sense of ownership and personal responsibility for the learning process.

SELF-REFERENCING AND FORCED-CHOICE ITEM DESIGN

With respect to assessment design, Coaley (2010), with a background in psychometrics, suggests that the benefits for the designer of self-referenced assessments or questionnaires are that all the hard work of creating norms is not needed. Conversely, limitations are, inevitably, that there is no comparison that can meaningfully be made with anyone else: 'ipsative questionnaires purely reflect variance within individuals and cannot tell us about variance between them' (Coaley, 2010: 65). To illustrate, an ipsative assessment statement would be: *Mary's interest in number is stronger this year than it was last year*, indicating variance over time, or *Mary's interest in number is stronger than her interest in reading*, indicating variance between fields. By comparison, a **norm-referenced** statement would be *Mary's interest in number is greater than most of her year group whereas her interest in reading is average within the same group*.

An example of ipsative test design is one that uses forced-choice items. The person taking the test has to choose the statement that best describes a particular aspect of his or her learning preferences from amongst a group of statements (normally three to five choices), any or all of which could in some way be true. A learning styles questionnaire could be designed in this way, for instance:

When you are solving problems, do you:

(a) take a trial and error approach?
(b) research the topic thoroughly before deciding which approach to take?
(c) ask the opinion of an expert?

The resulting scores correlate with the relative rank on each scale for each individual who undertakes the questionnaire. There is no one ranking based on a single scale for the total population of those undertaking it (see **measurement**).

In the lifelong learning sector, ipsative approaches are commonly associated with entry-stage **diagnostic** assessment and/or **self-assessment**. Individuals are encouraged to analyse their initial strengths and areas for further development and then to identify personal learning targets against which future progress will be assessed (Tummons, 2011). With adults in particular, the notion of ipsative assessment lies behind pedagogic techniques such as learning journals, reflection on practice and coaching.

FURTHER READING

Coaley, K. (2010). *An Introduction to Psychological Assessment and Psychometrics.* London: Sage.

Tummons, J. (2011). *Assessing Learning in the Lifelong Learning Sector* (3rd edn). Exeter: Learning Matters.

Mark Scheme

A mark scheme is a set of criteria used when assessing a piece of work in a test or assessment. It is usual to write the mark scheme at the same time as the assessment or question paper. It is also usual for the person setting the questions to write the mark scheme, and for the mark scheme to contain a rubric, or scoring tool. The rubric will set out how marks can be awarded. The rubric is the examiner's or assessor's first attempt to specify how marks can be gained. This will be finalised at a standardisation meeting. The criteria are linked to the learning objectives found in the specification upon which the test or assessment is based.

For each externally set assessment or question paper and for each internally set assessment, there must be a mark scheme that is designed to ensure that all examiners or assessors mark the assessment or question paper consistently and reliably. For internally set assessments, this is also considered good practice. The mark scheme provides the range of expected responses to all the questions in the question paper and indicates how many marks should be awarded to any particular answer or response. The marks for each question in the mark scheme must exactly match those in the question paper, which normally includes an indication of the mark allocation for each question or sub-question.

All mark schemes are intended to promote positive marking, i.e. it is assumed that a candidate starts with zero marks and is awarded marks for whatever achievement is demonstrated, rather than starting with a maximum number of marks and having marks deducted for wrong or incomplete answers. However, some professional organisations that also assess and accredit may subtract marks for wrong answers. If this happens, this should always be clearly stated, with reasons given for the subtraction of the mark and the purpose behind such an approach.

PRODUCING THE MARK SCHEME

The principal examiner for the external assessment or question paper is responsible for producing the associated mark scheme and is required to produce it at the same time as the question paper is being drafted. For an internal assessment, the person responsible for setting the assessment is the one who should produce the mark scheme, again, at the same time as the question paper is being developed. It allows the principal examiner to demonstrate that the question paper is actually testing what it is designed to test in terms of the assessment objectives, assessment criteria and subject content targeted by the question paper. In other words, this procedure ensures that it is valid in terms of the construct.

MARK SCHEME FORMAT

The format of the mark scheme depends on the nature of the question paper and what is being tested or assessed. Some mark schemes (or sections of mark schemes) award marks point by point. Candidates are awarded a mark for the correct answer (or for a correct response if there is more than one possible correct answer) and no marks for an incorrect answer. In some cases, the principal examiner will list a range of acceptable and unacceptable answers to offer guidance to the examining or assessment team.

For a more complex question, the mark scheme may allow a range of possible marks, depending on the accuracy and extent of the response. So, for example, a question marked out of three may allow the following: one mark for a correct response, two marks for a correct response plus a simple explanation, and three marks for a correct response plus a fuller explanation.

MARKING EXTENDED RESPONSES

For an extended response such as an essay or report, the mark scheme may take the form of levels of response. A range of levels is described using descriptors, which mirror the objectives that are assessed in the question. For each level, there is a range of marks; e.g. Level 1 = marks 1–5, Level 2 = marks 6–10, Level 3 = marks 11–15, and so on. Examiners or the assessment team have first of all to decide which level descriptors best fit the candidate's response and then to decide which mark within the range for that level is the most appropriate. The level of response is often linked to the command verb being used by the principal examiner – the more demanding the command word, the more marks are awarded. This concept is explored in more detail under **measurement** and its reference to Bloom's Taxonomy. Indicative content often accompanies a level of response mark scheme.

QUALITY OF WRITTEN COMMUNICATION

Where appropriate, mark schemes include instructions for the assessment of the quality of a candidate's written communication, which might include spelling, punctuation, grammar, clarity and expression. If these are to be assessed, this needs to be made explicit in both the specification and the mark scheme, otherwise the assessment runs the risk of not being valid, because the assessment is assessing something that is not part of the specification – in this case the ability to communicate accurately in written format. Technically this is termed construct irrelevance variance; it refers to an assessment assessing something it is not designed to do, e.g. assessing language skills in a mathematics paper.

The resulting scores will show a variance in marks, which will be attributable to something that the assessment was not designed to assess.

PROVISIONAL MARK SCHEMES

Mark schemes are reviewed and revised in conjunction with question papers throughout the question paper setting process. Provisional mark schemes are then provided to examiners shortly before their **standardisation** meeting so that they can familiarise themselves with the mark scheme before the meeting and attempt to apply it to a sample of candidates' responses. During this process, the mark scheme is often amended to accommodate candidates' responses which appear correct but which had not been anticipated. This will be finalised at the standardisation meeting. Once the mark scheme has been agreed at the standardisation meeting, this is noted and accepted as the final version – the one that all assessors who are marking the candidates' work will use. Such an approach allows for the assessment to be transparent, in other words it is clear to all participants in the process – the assessors and the candidates – how marks can be gained and how they have been attained.

PUBLICATION OF MARK SCHEMES

At the end of the standardisation and marking period, mark schemes are made available to schools and colleges, who may use them for marking mock examinations and/or to aid their understanding of the requirements of the question paper. By publishing the mark scheme, the assessors also make transparent their reasons for awarding marks or grades. In terms of professional development, there can be no substitute for attending the standardisation meeting to hear a full explanation of how the mark scheme is applied.

FURTHER READING

Chartered Institute of Educational Assessors (2007). *Mark Scheme*. Available at: http://www.ciea.co.uk

Kleinmann, M., Kuptsch, C. and Köller, O. (1996). 'Transparency: a necessary requirement for the construct validity of assessment centres'. *Applied Psychology*, 45 (1), 67–84.

mark scheme

> To measure something is to ascertain the extent or quantity of that thing by comparison with a fixed unit or with an object of known size. Measurement in assessment is usually defined as the act of assigning letters, numbers or symbols, according to a known, specific set of rules or to a standard.

A standardised instrument is generally used to measure how big, heavy, hot or long something is. When we measure something, we do not assess it; we simply collect information about it relative to some established and agreed standard: Celsius, metre, kilogramme. When we assess something, we collect information about a previously known and agreed objective. We often ascribe to this information a measurement in the form of a score or grade. If we are assessing a skill, the measurement is comparatively straightforward – either someone can perform the skill at an acceptable standard or not. However, if we wish to assess knowledge or understanding this becomes more problematic.

First, we need to determine what we are actually measuring. According to classical test theory (CTT), we need to determine the domain in which we are to operate. Krathwohl *et al.* (1964) articulated three separate domains that can help us to determine what we are to measure, commonly known as Bloom's Taxonomy. The domains are: cognitive, affective and psychomotor. The cognitive deals with intellectual capacities and our ability to think; the affective deals with feelings, emotions and attitudes; the psychomotor deals with physical skills and the ability to use technologies.

These taxonomies can be used as a checklist to determine what you are trying to assess. They are hierarchical and Krathwohl *et al* (1964) believed that one cannot progress to the next level within the hierarchy without mastery of the 'simpler' levels. These levels range, within the cognitive domain, from the ability to recall knowledge to the ability to evaluate; within the affective domain they range from the ability to receive information to the ability to internalise values; within the psychomotor

key concepts in educational assessment

domain they range from the ability to imitate the performance of others to the ability to perform activities and their related skills for strategic purposes.

Having determined which domain to measure, we need to determine the trait (characteristic) that will make up part of that domain. For example, we may wish to look at a learner's abilities in the domain of mathematics. We need to look first at a particular trait, say the ability to calculate the area of two-dimensional objects. We may ask a learner to calculate the area of a square or rectangle; we may then move on to relatively more difficult tasks such as the area of a triangle or the area of a circle. If we are to differentiate between different responses from learners, we need to consider:

- How many times do I need to ask the question about the calculation of the surface area of a two-dimensional object before I am confident that this learner understands the concept and can apply that understanding in different circumstances?
- How much 'weight' do I give to each question? That is to say, how many marks do I give the correct completion of the question? To help make assessment manageable, the fewer times we ask the type of question the better.

In terms of weighting, we need to consider Bloom's Taxonomy and determine the level of difficulty of the task we are setting. At the lower end of the cognitive domain hierarchy, we may wish to credit only one mark for a correct answer because the learner has simply had to recall the formula for calculating the area of a rectangle.

However, the task may involve more than one domain. We may ask a learner to calculate the area of a diagram that involves a multiple set of shapes and apply understanding to a variety of circumstances that cross all three domains simultaneously. For example, we may ask a learner to analyse the problem, apply his or her understanding in the cognitive domain, justify the actions within the affective domain and coordinate the activities within the psychomotor domain. This type of task would require more weight than that given to a simple calculation.

Further, we need to consider the type of scale to use. There are four types of measurement scale:

- the nominal scale, which simply offers different variables, such as 'engages with the task (or does not)'
- the ordinal scale, which gives a rank order but does not assign any value to the ranking, for example we may know that a score of four

is better than a score of two, but there is no implication that four is twice as good as two

- the interval scale, in which the distance between one point on the scale is exactly the same as another, for example the difference between four and five is exactly the same as the difference between five and six. However, a score of zero does not indicate that the thing being measured is absent. Both the Fahrenheit and Celsius temperature scales are examples of an interval scale
- the ratio scale, where zero is the complete absence of the thing being measured and four is worth twice as much as two and eight is twice as much as four.

Having decided upon scale, domain(s) and the traits we wish to measure, we need to make all of this clear both to other assessors and to the learners. This is normally achieved by describing the learning outcome (LO) that we are trying to measure. Learning outcomes are the specific intentions of a learning programme, module, unit or lesson and usually relate to what a learner knows, understands and can do within a particular domain.

The learning outcomes are accompanied by assessment criteria (AC). These are descriptions of what a learner must do in order to demonstrate that a learning outcome has been achieved. AC are usually accompanied by the weighting accorded to a particular question and by a description of indicative evidence that may fulfil the criteria. This is to help learners and assessors understand the nature of the task and how to fulfil it successfully.

The AC need to reflect the learning outcome being assessed. We need to work out what will constitute success and describe it using our selected scale. It may be necessary to describe a range of factors that will help both the learner and assessor to clarify the context and focus on what is essential in order to be confident that we have an appropriate measurement tool.

The assessors who will be making the assessment judgements need to be standardised and their work moderated.

PSYCHOMETRICS

However, how can we be sure that our measurement tool worked in the way we hoped it would? There is an entire field of theoretical study linked to the measurement of educational assessment known as psychometrics.

This involves the analysis of data that emanate from any assessment. Individual scores are analysed to find patterns across cohorts of students, so that different tests and assessments, administered similarly to different groups of students, can be placed on a single scale. This can be done for a single assessment or examination, or for single items within an assessment.

Much of the early work in psychometrics was done in an attempt to measure intelligence (see **intelligence quotient**). Francis Galton is often considered the father of psychometrics for his work in developing IQ tests. Later, L.L.Thurstone, the founder of the Psychometrics Society, developed a statistical method of describing variables. This has since developed into factor analysis, which describes variability among a set of observed and correlated variables in relation to other uncorrelated variables known as factors. Factor analysis is used to determine the different factors that may or may not have given the observed results in any given assessment.

This approach can help to determine not only the **reliability** of the assessment method you have chosen, but also its **validity**. A further approach can be used to determine the efficacy of the assessment we have set, using Item Response Theory (IRT), which uses mathematical models to ascertain the effectiveness of each of the items, or questions, or tasks, we have used within our assessment. IRT will also allow us to determine the efficacy of the measurement tool we have used, not only around each item, but also by looking at the assessment as a whole.

A further model that can be used is the Rasch measurement model, which measures traits within any domain. This is done by analysing all responses to an item within an assessment and determining the likelihood of a candidate's success in any particular question, by looking at responses to other questions and determining how others answered the same item. This allows the designer of the assessment to determine how difficult a question has been for the cohort and, correspondingly, how well any candidate has performed in any given item (Bond and Fox, 2001).

These mathematical models help assessors to determine the effectiveness of any assessments they have designed, whether a single item or the entire assessment, as well as the importance of any variables that may impact upon learners' performance. They also help the assessor to check for the reliability and validity of the assessment.

Impara, J. C. and Plake, B. S. (1996). 'Professional development in student assessment for educational administrators: an instructional framework'. *Educational Measurement: Issues and Practice*, 15 (2), 14–19.

McMillan, J. H. and Nash, S. (2000). *Teacher classroom assessment and grading practices decision making*, Annual Meeting of the National Council on Measurement in Education, New Orleans, LA.

Sanders, J. R. and Vogel, S. R. (1993). 'The development of standards for teacher competence in educational assessment of students'. In S. L. Wise (ed.), *Teacher Training in Measurement and Assessment Skills*. Lincoln, NE: Buros Institute of Mental Measurements, University of Nebraska–Lincoln.

Moderation

Moderation is the process through which assessment is monitored within an awarding organisation to ensure that it is reliable, fair and consistent with required standards.

THE MODERATION PROCESS

Along with the design of **mark schemes** and **standardisation**, moderation can be regarded as part of a sequence of events in a process that is designed to provide validity and reliability. Whereas standardisation is intended to ensure that individual assessors are applying similar standards, moderation is aimed at groups of assessors working together, at departments within institutions, or at institutions belonging to a group that together award a **qualification**. So, for example, a university or college that teaches the same subject on a number of different sites will require assessors on each site to be moderated so that grades can be awarded with consistency, no matter which site conducted the

key concepts in educational assessment

teaching and assessment for any given student. Similarly, a group of schools whose teachers assess a **coursework** or controlled assessment element that contributes towards an externally awarded qualification will be required by the awarding body to have the assessment decisions of their teachers verified by a moderator in order to ensure consistent standards.

METHODS OF MODERATION

An individual moderator, specifically appointed to that role, can undertake moderation, or moderation can refer to a process that takes place between peers engaged in the assessment process. Inter-assessor consistency can be achieved or improved by using trial marking and standardisation by the marking team. Additional methods include double-blind marking (where two examiners award a mark or grade without knowing the mark or grade awarded by the other). Double-blind marking creates an administrative load and institutions might prefer to attempt to achieve similar outcomes by single marking and judicious sampling. Sampling is where a moderator reviews a cross-section of a marker's work to standardise the marks awarded. When moderating assessment outputs across a large population of assessments, one can ensure consistency in results by using a statistical formula known as a scale factor. This ensures that the differences in scores remain the same on a pre-determined scale but can be adjusted if they are generally higher or lower than the required standard.

Group moderation is where a group of markers discuss examples of assessed work in order to share their understandings of the agreed criteria, and 'thus both the processes and products of assessment are considered' (Gipps, 2012: 63). External examiners, where they are appointed, also comment on assessment procedures and standards, thus enhancing or ratifying the moderation processes that have already taken place.

VERIFICATION

Among the awarding bodies for school examinations, one of the biggest changes over the last decade has been on-screen marking, which also allows for the moderation of markers during the process itself and the ability to pause, advise and even stop markers from working. Another big change is that awarding bodies use fewer and fewer moderation training meetings and have shifted over to online training.

Normally, the moderating process depends on verification rather than re-marking. Where two markers disagree, there is a temptation for a third marker to split the difference. Verification, as opposed to re-marking, would be more likely to use pendulum arbitration where the moderator decides which of the two proposed marks best fits the criteria set out in the mark scheme and the interpretations decided at standardisation.

The marking and moderation of school-based public examinations is anonymous in the sense that codes of practice prevent examiners from assessing schools with which they have personal or professional links. Therefore, while markers may see student names on scripts, the names should not mean anything to the marker. However, in some parts of the world, there may be a perception that markers might be biased against or in favour of students whose names reveal a particular characteristic such as gender, age or ethnicity, and whether or not this perception has a basis in reality, students might be identified on scripts by candidate numbers only.

Many university administrators appear to believe that anonymous marking is an aid to moderation. However, this is easier to implement in traditional closed-book examinations than it is in continuously assessed coursework. It is also difficult to achieve in small departments. Tutors might well believe that personal contact with the candidate is educationally preferable to anonymity due to the pedagogic aims of assessment for learning. They might also believe that plagiarism is reduced if the tutor–assessor can observe a student's work develop, and that anonymity reduces the ability of the assessor to keep track of and therefore vouch for the provenance of a piece of work submitted for assessment and moderation.

FURTHER READING

Brown, G., Bull, J. and Pendlebury, M. (1997). *Assessing Student Learning in Higher Education*. London: Routledge.

Ofqual (2011). *GCSE, GCE, Principal Learning and Project Code of Practice*. Coventry: Ofqual.

National Curriculum Assessment

England's 5- to 16-year-olds must follow a national curriculum that was introduced in 1988. While teachers assess most subjects, English and mathematics are externally assessed at the end of key stages through national curriculum tests, popularly known as SATs. Currently students take tests: at the end of Key Stage 1 in English and mathematics that are marked by teachers; at the end of Key Stage 2 in science that are marked by teachers and in English and mathematics that are mainly externally marked.

Until recently, a child in England entering the system at age 5 could sit as many as 105 formal assessments before he or she left formal education at 18, leading critics to complain that English students were the most over-assessed children in the world (National Union of Teachers, 2002). However, the pendulum has swung back to a certain extent.

In the early 1980s, the government was concerned about falling standards in schools and children's relatively poor basic skills (Machin and Vignoles, 2006) and therefore introduced a national curriculum in 1988 that defined what students should study. The Education Reform Act of 1988 authorised a testing regime that included assessing pupils at or near the end of each key stage in order to ascertain what they had achieved in relation to that key stage's attainment targets (Education Reform Act, 1988). Attainment targets spell out national expectations for performance through level descriptions on an eight-level scale. The average 7-year-old is expected to reach level 2 and the aim is to have students move up one level every two years.

Although initially students were assessed by a variety of different means including tests, practical tasks and observation (DES, 1987), the assessments proved time-consuming and burdensome and were reshaped in the early 1990s, moving away from teachers' control. Written **examinations** in English, mathematics and science taken by an entire year group were introduced that were shorter and externally marked (House of Commons, 2009).

In 1997 the government introduced assessment targets that mandated proportions of students to reach certain attainment levels and started to publish the results of the tests' outcomes. National newspapers published rank orders of schools based on test results, leading schools to scramble for ever higher places in national league tables.

National curriculum assessments are used for a variety of **purposes:** as a tool to raise standards; to ascertain individual students' progress; to judge individual teacher performance; to ascertain where intervention in a school is necessary; and to hold schools accountable (Stobart, 2008).

In May 2008, the parliamentary Children, Schools and Families Committee (CSFC) published a report on national testing that stated that 'national testing for school accountability has resulted in some schools emphasising the maximisation of test results at the expense of a more rounded education for their pupils' (House of Commons CSFC, 2008). It claimed that teaching to the tests was widespread, narrowing teaching to English, mathematics and science and in particular those aspects that were tested, which compromised teachers' creativity and children's access to a broad and balanced curriculum. While in principle supportive of national testing, it agreed with Newton's arguments that national curriculum tests were used for too many purposes (Newton, 2007a) and recommended that the system should uncouple the multiple purposes of measuring pupil attainment, school and teacher accountability and national monitoring (House of Commons CSFC, 2008).

A government-authorised review of national curriculum testing, led by Lord Bew, recommended retaining testing at Key Stage 2, with modifications to the marking of English writing tests (Bew Review, 2011). The current government then announced that it will review the national curriculum and its assessment for all key stages.

Tim Oates (2011), who led an expert group that advised the government on the 2011–2012 national curriculum review, writes about the delicate balance between the national curriculum and its complementary assessments. He argues for minimal, but clear specification of curricular aims, objectives and key content and concepts, stating that without these assessment becomes what he calls 'ambush assessment' because teachers might be unclear about what will appear on national tests. 'Frantic search, by teachers and parents, for past test papers thus ensues, and the curriculum degrades into "that which will be assessed"' (pp. 142–3). According to Oates, a poorly conceived curriculum can cause: over assessment – if the curriculum is too highly specified; an inability to develop fair assessments – if the curriculum is too general; inappropriate **discrimination** in assessments geared toward certain age groups – if the progression routes through the curriculum are unclear; loss of face **validity** – if the curriculum contains irrelevant content; and a narrowing of scope – if the curriculum does not enshrine deep learning.

CURRENT ASSESSMENT ARRANGEMENTS

Results from the consultation on the national curriculum review had not been announced before this book's publication. At the time of writing, the following assessment arrangements are in place.

Under the aegis of the Department for Education, the Standards and Testing Agency (STA) develops tests for Key Stages 1 and 2, as well as having responsibility for the Early Years Foundation Stage Profile, which assesses students prior to compulsory schooling. All national curriculum subjects are assessed each year through teachers making summary judgements against the attainment targets at the end of each key stage.

At the end of Key Stage 1, the emphasis is on teachers' judgements, but there are also externally set tests that teachers use in reading comprehension, writing (including spelling) and mathematics. The tests are marked within the school and schools decide when to administer them. All of the tests are **criterion-referenced** and contain a mix of selection and supply items. Schools must report a teacher-assessed level for each child in reading, writing, listening and speaking, mathematics and science, plus a separate teacher-assessed level for each science attainment target.

In 2012 the government introduced a new, statutory phonics screening check to be taken by all students in the first year of Key Stage 1 (at age 6). It is a test of phonic decoding and consists of 40 words that students read one-to-one to a teacher. Controversially, half of the words are 'non-words' and therefore unfamiliar. They are meant to allow fair assessment of students who have limited vocabulary knowledge and/or word memory. Examples of the non-words include tox, ulf, thazz and quemp (DfE, 2012).

Alongside teacher assessment, students must take statutory externally set and marked tests in mathematics and English at the end of Key Stage 2 as a key accountability measure for all primary schools. Up until 2009 they also had to take tests in science; national standards in science are now measured through a statutory sampling arrangement. In 2012 arrangements were put in place to rely on teachers' judgements of English writing, following Lord Bew's recommendation. Those judgements must be informed by the results of a writing test, which can be internally marked.

The English and mathematics tests are administered on set days. The tests are criterion-referenced and contain a mix of supply and select items. The English test consists of a one-hour reading test, a 10-minute spelling test and two writing tests – a 20-minute shorter task and a 45-minute longer one. Mathematics includes both mental mathematics and two 45-minute tests. A new statutory test of grammar, punctuation and spelling will be introduced for children at the end of Key Stage 2 from May 2013. It will consist of closed and short response items.

The average student at the end of Key Stage 2 is expected to reach level 4 and schools set and publish performance targets for the percentage of students who will achieve levels 4 and 5 (DCSF, 2009). Results of the tests are provided to parents and the public, and are used to judge school as well as student performance. Aggregated school data are used to form an overall picture of local and national attainment.

Students used to be assessed externally at the end of Key Stage 3 in English, mathematics and science but are now assessed by teachers' summative judgements across all subjects. Teachers must report each student's level of achievement for each attainment target in English, mathematics, science and modern foreign languages, as well as an overall subject level for each of the core and non-core subjects. An average student is expected to achieve at level 5 or 6 by the end of Key Stage 3. National curriculum assessment at Key Stage 4 is largely through GCSEs (see **qualifications**).

FURTHER READING

Daugherty, R. A. (1995). *National Curriculum Assessment: A Review of Policy, 1987–1994*. London: RoutledgeFalmer.

Machin, S. and Vignoles, A. (2006). *Education Policy in the UK*. London: Centre for Economics of Education, London School of Economics.

Norm referencing enables assessors to sort individuals across a range of abilities or aptitudes. Individual learning is evaluated and graded by judging each person's performance against that of a larger group of people in the same age group or at the same stage or level of learning. The larger group is known as the 'norm' or normative group.

An educational assessment procedure can be identified as norm-referenced when the score that an individual achieves is converted into a statement or grade indicating how that individual compares with others who have undergone the same assessment. This process is based on the assumption that the group of people being assessed share similar relevant characteristics across a spectrum or range. In compulsory education, the characteristics in common may be as broad as the age or year group.

In designing a test that is to be norm-referenced, raw scores from individuals taking the new test are compared with scores taken from a sample of people who have taken previous tests assessing the same constructs. This sample is used 'to establish expected scoring patterns' for the test (Wright, 2007: 14). Where data are gathered from large samples of particular population-types that have acquired the relevant learning outcomes being assessed, **standardisation** can be undertaken. Standardisation 'means only the test is uniform . . . that all examinees face the same tasks, administered in the same manner and scored in the same way' (Koretz, 2008: 23). It is a procedure by which educational assessment designers ascertain average, below and above average scores for the particular attribute being tested (although in some circumstances, **criterion-referenced** tests may also have average, below and above average scores).

Designers of norm-referenced assessments can produce norm tables that enable the conversion from raw score to normative score, act as a source of reference for interpretation of individual scores and indicate performance relative to the distribution of scores obtained by others.

Advice for designers and interpreters includes the caution that norm groups should always be relevant to the *purpose* of the assessment (Coaley, 2010). If this is not carefully managed, there is a danger of assessment results being misinterpreted and inferences made regarding aspects of learning or **attainment** that the assessment was not designed to address.

Proponents of norm referencing claim that it provides valuable information to selectors, for example, for further educational or occupational purposes, about the attainment of individuals being assessed. It thereby enables useful selection and/or educational planning decisions to be made that they claim benefit all educational stakeholders, that is to say, learners, teachers, educational institutions and society. A sub-set of norm referencing is cohort referencing. This is where a normative-type distribution of scores (average, above and below average) is applied only to the cohort in question and thus the actual pass grade might vary from cohort to cohort. An example would be the former 11+ exam taken by pupils in the UK to sort those going to grammar school from those going to technical or secondary modern schools. This was particularly controversial as the norms for girls and boys were not the same. The average marks of boys permitted to progress to grammar school were lower than those of girls.

Those who challenge the predominance of norm referencing in educational assessment might do so for a number of reasons. This might be from the perspective of **fairness**, or equality of opportunity, because they believe norms cannot be ascertained free of cultural bias such as gender, ethnicity, national context, micro or macro culture (Au, 2009), or from a related ideological perspective that norm-referenced approaches in our educational assessment culture contribute to the creation and maintenance of hegemonic, hierarchical social relationships. Attempts to address such critiques could be claimed, for instance, by those designing the Wechsler Adult Intelligence Test. This has been standardised in both the UK and the USA – the former a context where social class identifiers remain resonant, the latter a so-called 'classless society'. However, such claims are unlikely to convince adherents to a sociological critique of educational assessment conventions such as Paul Smeyers and Marc Depaepe. They describe norm referencing as 'an indication of closed-loop thinking and built-in conservatism'. They also assert that criterion referencing, where the assessed individual is purportedly judged only on his or her relative 'mastery in a selected domain' (Smeyers and Depaepe, 2008: 56) rather than in relation to others being similarly assessed, and against which norm referencing is usually compared and contrasted, is shaped by norm-referenced expectations.

FURTHER READING

Coaley, K. (2010). *An Introduction to Psychological Assessment and Psychometrics.* London: Sage.

Wright, R. J. (2007). *Educational Assessment: Tests and Measurements in the Age of Accountability.* New York: Sage.

Peer and Self Assessment

Peer assessment has been described as a variant of self-assessment that entails learners assessing the work of contemporaries. Peer and self assessment are deemed to contribute to the acquisition of meta-cognitive skills (learning to learn) in the learning process.

self assessment

peer and

Peer assessment is a sophisticated skill that can take time to acquire and master and this is one of the reasons it is much heralded but little used in many educational contexts. Conducted in pairs or groups, peer assessment is an activity where learners adopt the role of critical friend and benefit from sharing ideas and insights. It involves the sharing and sometimes the negotiation of assessment criteria and can lead to a deeper understanding of and engagement with the assessment tasks and processes and the learning required to achieve them.

Peer assessment can therefore offer significant benefits for learners and their teachers and its proponents justify the time and resources required to develop this approach. For instance, Sebba *et al.* (2008) undertook a systematic review of the research evidence on students in secondary schools in the UK of self and peer assessment. The key findings were: a significant increase in **attainment** across all subject groups was achieved, with these benefits not varying much between a wide range of subjects; self-esteem and self confidence were increased; learning to learn skills improved; target setting and objective clarification were enhanced; and there was little variation dependent on student characteristics (gender, ethnicity, prior attainment). Munns and Woodward (2006) also found improvement in hard-to-reach learners. It is clear why peer assessment attracts strong advocates, based on this kind of evidence.

In 2004, Black *et al.* stated, 'self and peer assessment make unique contributions to the development of students' learning. They secure aims that cannot be achieved in any other way' (2004: 12). These include: developing understanding of assessment criteria and processes; gaining a feel for standards and quality; enabling learners to monitor their own progress; developing meta-cognitive skills through a more reflective approach to learning; a greater sense of ownership, responsibility and confidence. Black *et al.* (2004) suggest that learning to undertake peer assessment can be a valuable way of acquiring the more difficult skill of self-assessment. They write about peer assessment as a bridging skill to self-assessment as well as being an important skill in its own right. This is because assessing the work of peers can act as a stimulus to improving one's own work; it provides exemplification of what to avoid and what to aspire to. Boud *et al.* (1999) and Gibbs and Simpson (2004) in separate studies with students in higher education, in Australia and the UK respectively, state that students took their own work for assessment more seriously when they knew it would be peer-assessed, and findings suggested that in some instances students found **feedback** from peers more meaningful than from tutors.

Alongside the benefits claimed for learners are those for teachers. These include: a shift of responsibility from teacher to learner; the affordance of time for the teacher to stand back from delivery and observe; higher levels of motivation and independence in learners, which reduces the need for people-management tactics versus teaching. In addition, peer feedback can be woven together with teachers' overall

key concepts in educational assessment

assessment for learning strategies. This can produce overall greater efficiency in class management, leaving time to think through how to challenge learners to extend their achievements.

LIMITATIONS

Given this rich evidence base, and its champions, it is noteworthy that so few teachers invest in this approach. And there are indeed significant pitfalls. These include that providing constructive feedback is a sophisticated skill in which the teachers themselves may not be secure. Good training and regular practice and feedback on feedback-giving are required. The social dynamics of who assesses whom require planning and forethought and learners may complain that the teacher is abdicating responsibility. There is also a danger that if it becomes a requirement rather than a voluntary activity, it may be undertaken at a cynical, procedural level. There is also a broader contextual issue of congruence with the overall culture and ethos, the social, emotional and resource conditions that prevail in the learning institution or environment in which peer and/or self-assessment are conceived and take place. For instance, a teacher wishing to implement such an approach but who is going against the grain of 'how things are done around here' risks isolation and ambush. To illustrate this, one might consider where a 'best and a worst fit' for peer assessment would be located. A best fit might be in the professional training of counsellors where listening and giving feedback form the content as well as the process through which effective learning in aspects of this domain can *only* take place in this way. A worst fit could arguably be any highly competitive and hierarchical context where non-cooperative behaviours are modelled at leadership level.

Difficulties associated with peer assessment might nevertheless be addressed by making sure learners understand the advantages and pitfalls of peer assessment and engage with aspects of its design to promote ownership. In this context, students would be trained either through practice sessions or watching demonstrations as exemplification and discussing these. Behavioural ground rules would be agreed and time and attention to issues of emotional intelligence given to support the building of trust and authentic, congruent behaviours. Group composition would be given careful forethought with the teacher retaining responsibility for the overall process. For instance, the teacher would observe interactions carefully and challenge any inappropriate behaviour. Finally, clear and accessibly crafted assessment criteria would be provided or co-designed and assessment criteria cross-referenced with exemplification material.

The above long list of optimal conditions, however well intended, also signals a cautionary note in the reading of the evidence behind research claims on the benefits of peer (and by extension, self) assessment. Tan (2004) countered claims that self-assessment enhances student autonomy by proposing that it can have a disempowering and disciplinary effect. And contrary to reassurances given above by Sebba *et al.* (2008), Van Gennip, and colleagues suggest that interpersonal and structural variables have not yet been fully researched and that the evidence to date is therefore too thin to support the beneficial 'learning outcome' claims resting upon it (2009: 54). However, if the overarching purpose for peer and self-assessment is to enable learners to gain deeper insight into how to learn and to prepare for success in whatever field, it can be used to good effect.

FURTHER READING

Munns, G. and Woodward, H. (2006). 'Student engagement and student self-assessment: the REAL framework'. *Assessment in Education: Principles, Policy & Practice*, 13 (2), 193–213.

Sebba, J., Crick, R. D., Yu, G., Lawson, H., Harlen, W. and Durant, K. (2008). *Systematic review of research evidence of the impact on students in secondary schools of self and peer assessment. Technical report.* London: EPPI-Centre, Social Science Research Unit, Institute of Education, University of London.

Performance-based Assessment

Performance-based assessment is a test of the ability to apply knowledge, skills and understanding, usually in a real-life setting.

Educational assessment criteria related to judging complex and authentic performance-based assessment were proposed in the USA and defined as a set of standards (AERA, APA and NCME, 1999) linked to the following definition: 'Performance assessments: product- and behaviour-based measurements based on settings designed to emulate real-life contexts or conditions in which specific knowledge or skills are actually applied' (p. 179).

Gipps (2012: 10) stresses that an important feature of performance-based assessment is that by 'aiming to model the real learning activities that we wish pupils to engage with, for example written communication skills and problem-solving activities … assessment does not distort instruction'.

Performance assessment is an alternative to traditional methods of assessing student achievement. While traditional assessment requires students to answer questions correctly, often through a multiple-choice test or through a written response of some kind, performance assessment requires students to demonstrate knowledge and skills, including the process by which they solve problems, in a defined context. Performance assessments measure skills such as the ability to integrate knowledge across domain fields, contribute to the work of a group (see **group assessment**), or develop a plan of action when confronted with a new situation. Performance assessment, largely through portfolio assessment, was very popular in the USA during the 1990s. It was seen as a way of including disadvantaged students in appropriate assessment activities; students from ethnic minority groups and those with English as a second language were thought to benefit from such an assessment, although that proved not necessarily to be the case (Linn *et al.*, 1991; Koretz *et al.*, 1994).

One key feature of all performance assessments is that they require students to be active participants. They focus attention on how a student arrives at an answer as well as focusing on the answer itself. For example, students can display their knowledge of financial services by looking to arrange a loan to buy a car or something similar. They will have to investigate the kinds of offers available from banks, insurance companies and credit companies for people of their age. Finally, they must determine the best deal for them. Thus, the student must show an understanding of finances, interest rates, loan periods, and so on. Included in this would be the application of their understanding of mathematics, insurance and budgeting.

Pedagogy must be altered to incorporate knowledge and understanding as well as skills into practical applications. With carefully stated learning outcomes, performance-based assessment allows students to assess their own and their peers' performances more accurately and make more explicit the purpose of their learning.

However, performance-based assessment has disadvantages that have for the most part seen its abandonment in large-scale assessments. Performance-based assessments are difficult to design and can be subject to both construct irrelevance and under-representation, because they are assessing skills and knowledge not essential to the domain and/or cover limited aspects of the domain (Koretz, 2008). It has proved very difficult in practice to determine what represents a poor, average or excellent performance, since there are fewer questions and the necessary skills can come from a variety of subject domains. The assessments are time-consuming, which it could be argued, takes away from teaching time. A further issue is that evaluations are often subjective and the criteria for success are difficult to both determine and to agree; inter-rater reliability is an issue, even with detailed **mark schemes**. Consequently, assessment outputs are difficult to **standardise** and **moderate**. Further, such assessments are difficult for those with disabilities and those who attend schools with poor resources.

Many of the issues relating to performance-based assessment in the USA have been outlined by Koretz (2008). Elsewhere, performance-based assessment is closely identified with the arts and creative industries and usually manifests itself as practical assessments linked to **coursework,** portfolios and final **examinations,** in such contexts as music performances, dance repertoires, presentations of art work as a portfolio, and so on.

Other educational and training situations may relate to practical performance-based examinations of **vocational assessment** tasks, such as passing a driving test to obtain a licence, or performing a practical welding exam to obtain a vocational qualification as a welder. Yet there is no agreed single definition of either performance-based or performance-related assessment. Palm (2008) argues that there are two distinct categories that define performance assessment: *response-centred* and *simulation-centred.* The response-centred performance assessment model relates student responses to tasks such as written assessments and this could include assessments usually associated with more traditional forms of assessment such as cloze 'word completion' tests, as well as online multiple-choice responses to some form of **e-assessment.**

Simulation-centred performance-based assessment can include observation of actual student performance using specialist equipment beyond the usual paper and pencil tests. This can relate to authentic assessment activities that focus on high fidelity simulations where assignments are directly linked to **measurement** of real-life tasks as part of a vocational sector curriculum, in, for example, construction, plumbing, hairdressing, and so on.

FURTHER READING

Adamson, F. and Darling-Hammond, L. (2010). *Beyond Basic Skills: The Role of Performance Assessment in Achieving 21st Century Standards of Learning.* Stanford, CA: Stanford Center for Opportunity Policy in Education.

Linn, R. L., Baker, E. L. and Dunbar, S. B. (1991). 'Complex, performance-based assessment: expectations and validation criteria'. *Educational Researcher,* 20 (8), 15–21.

Purposes of Assessment

Educational assessments have multiple purposes, some of which have the potential to conflict with each other. In the 1990s the main purposes of educational assessment were defined as: to support learning (formative); to aid progression, certification or transfer (summative); and for accountability (summative). Recently, people have begun to question the stark distinction between formative and summative purposes, arguing that summative results can be used in many ways, including some formative uses. Paul Newton has defined over 20 educational assessment purposes. He and others have highlighted the dangers of using assessments for purposes for which they were not intended, which can lead to the undermining both of the assessment itself and of student learning.

In 1994 Wynne Harlen (cited in Broadfoot, 2007) defined assessment as the process of, first, gathering evidence, and second, interpreting that evidence in the light of some defined criterion in order to form a judgement. So at its most basic, the purpose of an educational assessment is to make a judgement or decision, but that simple statement hides many complexities. What tool or instrument is being used to make that decision? Is it technically sound? How is the decision going to be used – to feed back to learners so they understand what they need to do, to ascertain whether they can progress to the next challenge, to conclude whether they are qualified to enter a particular profession? Should assessment outcomes be used to make decisions about students, teachers, headteachers, schools, regional or national education authorities, or even the government itself? And should the social consequences of those decisions be included when ascertaining purposes?

Stobart (2008) stated that three fundamental questions about the use of any educational assessment need to be asked:

1 What is the principal purpose of the assessment?
2 Is the form of the assessment fit for purpose?
3 Does it achieve its purpose?

Mansell and James (2009) argue that because assessment is so critical in people's lives, it is necessary to distinguish between the intended uses of an assessment and the actual uses to which it is put.

In *Testing, Friend or Foe*, Black (1998) stated that the three main purposes of educational assessment were:

• to support learning
• to aid progression, certification or transfer
• for accountability.

He labelled the first formative (see **assessment for learning**) and the second and third summative (see **assessment of learning**). The absolute distinction between the two terms has been questioned over the last decade, with formative lately viewed as a purpose/use and summative viewed as a judgement about an assessment outcome. Newton (2007a) defined assessment judgements and uses in the following manner: judgements form a continuum from summative (appraisal, usually quantitative) to descriptive (analysis, usually qualitative). An example of the former is how well a student did compared to all other students in the group; an example of the latter how well a student understood a concept. Summative results can be used in many ways, including formative. Newton (2007a) distinguishes over 20 uses of educational assessment, many of which were encapsulated in a QCA submission to the House of Commons Children, Schools and Families Committee in 2008, as seen in Table 1.

Table 1 Uses of educational assessment

social evaluation	to judge the social or personal value of students' achievements
formative	to identify students' proximal learning needs, guiding subsequent teaching
student monitoring	to decide whether students are making sufficient progress in attainment in relation to expectations or targets; and, potentially, to allocate rewards or sanctions
diagnosis	to clarify the type and extent of students' learning difficulties in light of well-established criteria, for intervention
provision eligibility	to determine whether students meet eligibility criteria for special educational provision
screening	to identify students who differ significantly from their peers, for further assessment
segregation	to segregate students into homogeneous groups, on the basis of aptitudes or attainments, to make the instructional process more straightforward
guidance	to identify the most suitable courses, or vocations for students to pursue, given their aptitudes
transfer	to identify the general educational needs of students who transfer to new schools
placement	to locate students with respect to their position in a specified learning sequence, to identify the level of course which most closely reflects it
qualification	to decide whether students are sufficiently qualified for a job, course or role in life – that is, whether they are equipped to succeed in it – and whether to enrol them or to appoint them to it
selection	to predict which students – all of whom might, in principle, be sufficiently qualified – will be the most successful in a job, course or role in life, and to select between them
licensing	to provide legal evidence – the licence – of minimum competence to practice a specialist activity, to warrant stakeholder trust in the practitioner
certification	to provide evidence – the certificate – of higher competence to practise a specialist activity, or subset thereof, to warrant stakeholder trust in the practitioner
school choice	to identify the most desirable school for a child to attend

(Continued)

Table 1 (Continued)

institution monitoring	to decide whether institutional performance – relating to individual teachers, classes or schools – is rising or falling in relation to expectations or targets; and, potentially, to allocate rewards or sanctions
resource allocation	to identify institutional needs and, consequently, to allocate resources
organisational intervention	to identify institutional failure and, consequently, to justify intervention
programme evaluation	to evaluate the success of educational programmes or initiatives, nationally or locally
system monitoring	to decide whether system performance – relating to individual regions or the nation – is rising or falling in relation to expectations or targets; and, potentially, to allocate rewards or sanctions
comparability	to guide decisions on comparability of examination standards for later assessments on the basis of cohort performance in earlier ones
national accounting	to 'quality adjust' education output indicators

Source: House of Commons Children's, Schools and Families Committee, 2008: 16

It is easy to see from the above that the same educational assessment might be used for multiple purposes, which can lead to problems and undermine the assessment's original purpose. For example, although the tests associated with the US No Child Left Behind Act of 2001 were meant to improve children's abilities in mathematics, English and science (student monitoring), they are also used to determine federal funding for state education systems (system monitoring), which has had the perverse outcome of states developing tests that are of differing difficulty in order to maximise the number of students passing them (Linn *et al.*, 2002).

In the UK, it could be argued that the GCSE's main purpose should be for qualification and programme evaluation, but it is also put to many other uses, including student monitoring, guidance, selection, school choice, institution monitoring and system monitoring. If a school's funding and place in a performance table depends on how many of its students get GCSE grades A* to C in certain subjects, school staff are unlikely to view the qualification solely in terms of whether or not students will be sufficiently equipped for their roles in later life. Rather, they might be tempted to concentrate on students believed to be on the grade C/D border rather than on all students.

Because an assessment is fit for a certain purpose does not mean it will be fit for other purposes, and there have been calls among educators and some policy makers to implement a wider range of assessments so that assessments meant to gauge individual students' needs are not undermined by trying to use them for accountability purposes. In Scotland, France, Germany, Italy, Japan and Sweden, national sampling regimes are used for monitoring purposes, which provide an opportunity to gauge accurately whether students are progressing overall without making judgements about individuals. Using assessment outcomes judiciously could help to rebalance the curriculum/assessment equation.

FURTHER READING

Newton, P. E. (2010). 'The multiple purposes of assessment'. In B. McGraw, P. E. Peterson and E. L. Baker (eds), *International Encyclopedia of Education* (3rd edn). Maryland Heights, MO: Elsevier Science.

Taras, M. (2005). 'Asessment – summative and formative – some theoretical reflections'. *British Journal of Educational Studies*, 53 (4), 466–78.

Qualifications

The UK uses an unusual system of certificating achievement for upper secondary students, awarding separate subject-based qualifications rather than the internationally more common school leaving certificate. General Certificates of Secondary Education (GCSE) and General Certificates of Education Advanced Level (A level) are the most common secondary qualifications in England, Wales and Northern Ireland. These qualifications contain both external and internal assessment, although the former dominates in most subjects. Qualifications are highly regulated through qualifications and subject criteria and codes of practice.

The UK's system of awarding separate subject qualifications – the end point of a course of study leading to a certificate of accomplishment in a particular area – is an unusual practice. More commonly a country (or region) issues an inclusive school leaving certificate or a diploma when students finish post-compulsory education that covers more than one subject area and is used for entry to higher education or employment (Boyle, 2008; Le Métais, 2002).

In England, the modern public qualifications system can be traced back to 1836 when universities began setting examinations for school leavers. In 1918 the Secondary Schools Examinations Council introduced the Higher School Certificate, which resembled modern school leaving certificates in other countries, in that students had to pass examinations in a number of subjects in order to obtain it (Tattersall, 2007). Because of disquiet that able candidates were failing to obtain the Higher School Certificate because of weaknesses in only a few areas, the General Certification of Education (GCE) was introduced in 1951. The examinations were divided into Ordinary Level (O level) for 16-year-olds and Advanced Level (A level) for 18-year-olds.

Certificates of Secondary Education (CSE) were introduced in 1965 to provide for lower ability 14- to 16-year-olds. In 1988 O levels and CSEs were replaced by the General Certificate of Secondary Education (GCSE), which catered to an even wider ability range (Isaacs, 2010). A variety of vocationally related qualifications is also available to 14- to 19-year-olds. The government measures its success in upper secondary education by the number of qualifications 16- and 18-year-olds achieve and how well they do in them, which has led to ever-increasing government regulation and involvement (see Wolf, 2009, for a more detailed discussion).

By introducing qualifications for separate subjects, the UK shifted from a curriculum-led system to an examinations-led one. Qualifications' examination papers are externally set, administered under controlled conditions and marked by the **awarding body**. Internal assessment is limited to **coursework** and controlled assessment. Most academic qualifications have limited internal assessment; vocational qualifications are predominantly internally assessed (Isaacs, 2010). Other OECD nations mainly use external assessments in their **examinations**, such as Denmark, Estonia, Greece, Ireland, Latvia, Netherlands, Poland and Slovenia. Those that rely more on internal assessment include Japan, Korea, Queensland, South Australia, Spain, Sweden, Switzerland and Turkey.

Most states, however, have some form of controls in place to ensure standardisation (Boyle, 2008).

In England, Wales and Northern Ireland, most 14- to 16-year-olds take GCSEs, which are graded A* through G, although only a grade of A* to C is considered a good pass. The average number of GCSEs taken is about eight (BBC, 2008b), generally including English, mathematics and science, because schools are judged by how many students obtain five or more GCSEs grades A* to C, including English and mathematics. In 2011 58.3% of pupils achieved five good GCSEs (or the equivalent) at grade A* to C, including mathematics and English (DfE, 2011b). In 2011 a new accountability measure, the English baccalaureate, was introduced that measures achievement in English, mathematics, science, foreign language and humanities. Simply by publicly reporting out how many students achieved five A* to C grades in all five subjects caused schools to increase the number of their students taking those subjects from 22% in 2010 to 47% in 2013 (DfE, 2011b).

Post-16 students mostly study level 3 qualifications, which include Advanced Subsidiary (AS), A levels and a wide variety of vocational and vocationally related qualifications. Most students take four or more AS levels, which is a free-standing qualification comprised of the first half of an A level, in year 12 and complete three or more A levels in year 13. A levels are graded A* through E and the pass rate is over 90%. Both GCSEs and A levels are criterion-referenced. Since 2000 all A levels have been modularised and contain between four and six units. In 2012 the government announced that it was seeking to curtail the number of modules sharply in favour of larger assessments taken at the end of the course.

Both GCSEs and A levels include internal and external assessment. Typically a GCSE will have 25% internal assessment, originally referred to as coursework but now, more tightly defined and managed, as controlled assessment. Controlled assessment regulations spell out the rules for how each subject's assessment is set, the conditions under which it is taken and how it is marked. In all cases, some of the assessment is taken under strictly supervised conditions. Some GCSEs in more applied subjects have 60% controlled assessment; some, such as mathematics, have none at all. A typical A level will have 25–30% internal assessment, but some have none at all and more applied ones will have up to 67% internal assessment. The current government has questioned the need for coursework in A levels. Vocational qualifications typically have little, or no, external assessment.

Subject criteria set out the aims and learning outcomes, knowledge, understanding, skills and assessment objectives common to all specifications in that subject and provide the framework within which awarding bodies create specifications. Those specifications must also meet the regulators' general requirements, including the common and qualification criteria. Subject criteria are intended to ensure comparability and rigour, facilitate progression and help higher education and employers know what has been studied and assessed (QCA, 2004). As part of proposed A level reforms, the main purpose of which is to give universities far more input into A level content and assessment, the Office of Qualifications and Examinations Regulation (Ofqual) proposed in 2012 to end subject criteria for key A level subjects; instead awarding bodies would work with universities to produce qualifications that, within certain design parameters, 'could be distinctly different for different subjects, reflecting the needs of particular subject communities' (Ofqual, 2012a: 12).

Qualifications criteria are very specific about assessment arrangements and require awarding bodies to use a variety of question types and tasks, including extended writing, and assess the quality of written communication (Ofqual, 2011).

Most qualifications aimed at 14- to 19-year-olds are also governed by codes of practice, the aims of which are to promote quality, consistency, accuracy and fairness in the assessment and awarding of qualifications, as well as help maintain standards across specifications both within and between awarding bodies and from year to year. To achieve this, the codes set out principles and practices for the assessment and quality assurance of qualifications; the roles and responsibilities of awarding bodies and centres; and the requirement of a high-quality examination process (Ofqual, 2011). Ofqual uses the codes of practice to monitor awarding body practice and has the power to intervene if it judges that standards are not being upheld.

Regulation has meant that specifications tend to look very much the same from one awarding body to the next because the content, assessment methods and assessment weightings are so tightly specified, and possibly because awarding bodies do not want to jeopardise their market share. External assessments do not vary much from year to year and internal assessments are now also the subject of precise rules. Wolf (2009) argues that the qualifications system has become moribund as 'government places ever more barriers in the way of entry, innovation, and flexibility'.

FURTHER READING

Isaacs, T. (2010). 'Educational assessment in England'. *Assessment in Education: Principles, Policy & Practice*, 17 (3), 315–34.

Tattersall, K. (2007). 'A brief history of policies, practices and issues relating to comparability'. In P. Newton, J. A. Baird, H. Goldstein, H. Patrick and P. Tymms (eds), *Techniques for Monitoring the Comparability of Examination Standards* (pp. 42–96). London: QCA.

Quality Assurance

> Quality Assurance (QA) is the systematic monitoring and evaluation of the processes involved in developing a product or service, in this case, assessment. It maximises the probability that minimum standards of quality will be delivered.

Quality assurance (QA) is the process of determining whether products or services meet or exceed customer expectations. QA incorporates design, development, production and service. The most popular tool used to determine quality assurance is the Shewhart Cycle, developed by Dr W. Edwards Deming (1994), consisting of four steps: Plan, Do, Check, and Act (PDCA). The four QA steps within the PDCA model stand for:

- Plan: establish the objectives and processes required to deliver the desired results
- Do: implement the process
- Check: monitor and evaluate the process by testing the results against the predetermined objectives
- Act: apply actions necessary for improvement if the results require changes.

PDCA's goal is to ensure that excellence is inherent in every component of the process.

quality assurance

113

The Chartered Institute of Educational Assessors (CIEA) has used the PDCA cycle in its Professional Framework of Assessment. There are three basic steps:

- preparing for assessment
- conducting assessment
- feeding back after assessment.

The processes have been apportioned to different roles within the system, so that individuals involved in the assessment process can determine what each person should be doing at any stage (CIEA, 2009). These functions have been further described by the following:

- what the function is about – for example, designing assessments and assessment criteria
- what the function consists of – for example, designing the specification, or interpreting its assessment requirements
- who performs the task – for example, a principal examiner in an external assessment, or a head of subject in an internal assessment
- the outcomes delivered – the specification itself, the question papers or the mark scheme
- key indicators of performance – for example, taking responsibility for choosing the assessment instrument, meeting the agreed requirements, ensuring the levels of **reliability** or **validity** within the assessment
- delivering to an agreed schedule – ensuring that the work is completed in a timely manner
- individual competencies that can be expected of someone working at a predetermined level – the ability to design a specification, to choose an appropriate assessment instrument, proofreading skills, the ability to manage staff meetings, ICT skills, where appropriate
- enabling knowledge – the knowledge that is required to work in the assessment team, such as subject specialism, assessment methodology (CIEA, 2009).

HOW DOES QA WORK IN PRACTICE?

For each step of the process, it is possible to monitor activities and to evaluate the efficacy of actions. Thus for preparing for assessment, we check that activities have been carried out to ensure the reliability, validity and equity required. We ensure that the specification has met all regulatory requirements and that a sufficiently large team exists to run the assessment and the expected response from learners. We check for a named person responsible for the quality assurance of the task.

For the conducting of assessment, we record the **standardisation** process; there is someone responsible for ensuring that it is followed consistently; and an agreed mark scheme is adopted.

Once assessors have been standardised, monitor how they are applying the **mark scheme** to their scripts. If someone is consistently harsh or lenient, the assessor can be asked to alter scores. If, however, an assessor proves to be inconsistent, we ask for the whole batch to be remarked. By assessing online, we monitor this process in real time and stop assessors from assessing if their performance falls below the expected standard of accuracy.

We then concentrate on **feedback** both to the learner and to the rest of the assessment team. The latter is often completed with the use of statistical data. Feeding back to the learner can be affected more easily by following an agreed pattern, so that all learners understand the actions needed to improve, allowing the learner to close the gap between current and desired performance.

Feedback is most effective when:

- it is clearly linked to the learning intention
- the learner understands the success criteria
- it focuses on the task rather than the learner.

In carrying out these processes, individuals can determine not only their own effectiveness and monitor their own work, but also the effectiveness of the entire team.

USING STATISTICAL DATA

Many organisations use statistical process control (SPC) to predict levels of inaccuracy. SPC is the application of statistical methods to the monitoring and control of a process to ensure it operates consistently and predictably to produce an assessment. For example, we may set a reliability benchmark that can be determined by analysing the results of the assessment across different cohorts and across time. If reliability falls below a pre-determined level, then statistical models can be used to change the assessment outputs. At each point in the process, data relating to the production of accurate procedures is collected and used to predict future accuracy.

The quality of the service is dependent upon that of the assessors involved in the process, some of which is sustainable and effectively controlled, such as the standardisation procedure, while some is not, such as the level of tiredness of an assessor at any given time.

If the specification does not reflect the true quality requirements, the product's quality cannot be guaranteed. For instance, the scope for an assessment in level 2 mathematics should cover not only the mathematical requirements expected of a cohort working at level 2, but also the language requirements of the assessment at this level. If the language skills needed to interpret the questions in the mathematics assessment are at a higher level than the mathematics being assessed, we have to ask ourselves what is being assessed – the mathematics or the use of language (Koretz, 2008)?

Some **vocational assessment** has been linked to the International Organisation for Standards (ISO) in an attempt to describe the standards expected at various stages in the assessment process and to give international credibility to the QA process.

FURTHER READING

Chartered Institute of Educational Assessors (CIEA) (2009). *CIEA Professional Framework*. Available at: http://www.ciea.co.uk

Deming, W. E. (1994). *The New Economics for Industry, Government, Education*. Cambridge, MA: Massachusetts Institute of Technology, Center for Advanced Engineering Study.

Recording and Tracking

The recording of assessment evidence can be carried out in a variety of formats. Information should be recorded in a standardised way so that the data can be analysed and interrogated easily using a standard software package. Generally, the purposes of collecting and collating the information are threefold:

- informing the monitoring and evaluation of the planning of learning
- supporting both teaching and learning
- reporting the outputs and outcomes of the assessment, both for individual learners and for groups of learners.

It is important to bear in mind the purposes to which the data will be put when devising a method of collecting and collating the data.

RECORDING

Recording is a process of capturing data or transforming information to a format stored on a storage medium often referred to as a record. Historical records of events have been made for thousands of years in one form or another. Ways of recording text suitable for direct reading includes writing it on clay or slate and later on paper. However, other forms of data storage are easier for automatic retrieval, but we need a tool to read them. Printing a text stored in a computer allows for keeping a copy on the computer and also having a copy that is readable without a tool.

Technology continues to provide many means to represent, record and express ideas about a number of issues. A standard software package such as Excel will record data from assessments in an easily identifiable format that can be analysed and interrogated by the user. Often these are in the form of tables that include the learner's name and other uniquely identifiable fields. Learners can also be put into common groups such as classes or sets. How these tables are organised usually depends upon historic circumstances, but the purpose of collecting and collating these tables needs to be borne in mind if they are to be fit for this purpose.

TRACKING

Tracking in the sense of recording refers to the monitoring of learners' progress over time and ensuring that an individual remains on track to achieve a predetermined goal. The goal or objective for the learner is based upon previous **attainment** and is usually linked to easily identifiable attainment levels such as national curriculum levels of attainment in England or levels of attainment linked to an external assessment system or **examination** performance.

Thus if a learner is working at level 3, we would expect that learner to move on to level 4 work and secure that level over a known period of time, for example one academic year. The evidence set out in the recording process can take a variety of forms from informal notes on planning to group records in relation to the learning objectives and pupils' work, including the marking comments on this work. If the objectives in the medium term are pitched appropriately for each learner and reflect the progression that each learner has made, then evidence of attainment against these objectives will show the extent to which learners are on track to achieve their longer-term targets. These could be end-of-year targets or end of key stage targets in a school, or they could be end of unit attainments in a modular course at college.

RECORDING AND TRACKING IN PRACTICE

The ways in which these medium-term plans are written will vary from institution to institution and from subject area to subject area. Some subjects, particularly within the English compulsory education system, have teaching and learning objectives for each year group that are designed to reflect the prescribed curriculum. These objectives provide a focus for the setting of individual targets, for medium-term plans and for a vocabulary with which to discuss and agree attainment and progress. If learners are working at levels that can be reasonably expected of someone in a particular year group, then learners and their teachers can claim that the work is at the level of national expectations. If learners are working at levels of work beyond national expectations, then they can claim to be working above the expectations of that particular year group. Similarly, if they are working below national expectations, then detailed records need to be kept to show that these learners are in fact making progress, despite the fact that they are not working where they should reasonably expect to be. It is usual for institutions to flag these attainments using a colour-coded system: a standard format for learners working at expected levels, green formatting for those working and attaining beyond expectations and red formatting for those working below the expected level (AIAA, 2007).

Indications of attainment and progress in relation to these learning objectives in medium-term planning will be expressed in curriculum terms. This can be quantified metrically. For example, 70% of the learners in a cohort are working at the level of national expectations, whereas 25% are working above those expectations and 5% are working below them. When learners display either above or below expectations in attainment, then changes need to be made to medium-term plans for both teaching and learning. These need to be recorded and changes to planning and delivery highlighted by both teachers and learners.

In the longer term, the data collected from learners' progress that reflect programmes of study can be recorded as specific levels or scores that can be translated into marks for examinations. Summarising levels on an annual basis requires something more from the data. It requires the data to reflect national curriculum levels or marks to add to examination performance. This often requires results to be graded within a level or grade band. Many institutions therefore use a lettering system – a, b, c – to denote how secure the scoring is. Using such **grading**, however, poses difficulties for the practitioner. Levels or grades represent a summation of scores at the end of a period of study, while the internal grading of scores reflects the learner's progress over the shorter term; they may also reflect a learner's progress in one particular strand of the whole.

A summative judgement may well represent a learner's progress and show a linear, steady development. However, learning is not necessarily linear. It is characterised by spurts of progress followed by periods of consolidation. Any recording and tracking system needs to take this into account.

REPORTING

Effective recording and tracking of learners' progress can also help when compiling summative reports to stakeholders. These stakeholders could be the assessment team itself – those people involved with the cohort of learners. By interrogating the data, it is possible to determine which assessments worked effectively and which did not. Some assessments can therefore be reused and others discarded as not fit for purpose.

Other stakeholders may include senior management teams that will wish to use the data to ensure that learners are on track for achieving what is expected of them and that any interventions taken with specific groups of learners have proved to be effective. It will also help senior managers to remain accountable for their provision. The data, if used effectively, can also help in the reporting of summative data to parents and carers, letting them know how their children are performing individually and against national expectations. The data will also help them to support staff in their intervention programmes if these have been initiated.

Employers may find this information useful, especially if it relates to vocational courses, showing them the kinds of attainment of which learners in the local community are capable. Many employers sit on governing bodies or as members of a board of trustees and can help the institution in its accountability.

Effective recording and tracking of learners following assessment can provide a rich source of information that can be used for a variety of purposes.

FURTHER READING

AIAA (2007). *Recording and tracking pupils' attainment and progress: the use of assessment evidence at the time of inspection.* Available at: http://www.aaia.org.uk/pdf/publications

Ofsted (2010). *The Annual Report of Her Majesty's Chief Inspector of Education, Children's Services and Skills 2009/10.* Available at: http://www.ofsted.gov.uk/resources/annual-report-of-her-majestys-chief-inspector-of-education-childrens-services-and-skills-200910

Regulation of Assessment

key concepts in educational assessment

Countries in the UK have an unusual regulatory system that governs the development, accreditation and awarding of national curriculum tests and qualifications. The purpose of regulation is to ensure tests and qualifications are fit for purpose, fair and of a secure standard. Regulation is also meant to ensure public confidence in testing and qualifications systems.

Regulation, that is, rules and legal actions governments take on behalf of the public good, is commonly associated with economic regulation, for example the regulation of public utilities. Its aim is to avoid conflicts between service providers and the people who use services and to guarantee that safe and appropriate services are delivered without unduly hampering business functions. Regulation of educational provision also concerns safe delivery of educational services, but is more associated with government oversight of quality and standards (Nisbet and Greig, 2007b). Government control is seen as necessary to attain educational excellence and to hold schools and teachers accountable through centralised curricula and testing (Scoppio, 2002).

Worldwide, it is common for governments, either nationally or regionally, to regulate what students are taught through common curricula, but the regulation of assessment varies. The commonest regulation method is the delivery of secondary school leaving certificates that reflect recipients' achievements in high-stakes formal assessment. This is usually administered or tightly regulated nationally by the state, for example in France and Italy. In some countries, individual regions take on this function, for example Australia, Canada and Germany, often with national agreements over standards. Many nations also legislate systems of national testing both at primary and secondary levels, for example Singapore. In the USA, No Child Left Behind legislation mandates that individual states develop, implement and regulate tests for both primary and secondary students.

Each constituent country in the UK has regulated systems of **national curriculum assessment**, but there is also a fairly unusual regulatory arrangement of accrediting and awarding separate **qualifications** for individual subjects within a qualifications framework rather than the issuance of a school-leaving certificate. The following concentrates on England, the most highly regulated of the countries in the UK.

When A and O levels were introduced in England in 1951, there were many providers – **awarding bodies** – of qualifications; in the vocational arena there were many more. By the late 1980s, there were major concerns about accountability, coherence and standards, which led to the introduction of the national curriculum. At the same time, the General Certificate of Education (GCSE) began. The newly created Schools Examinations and Assessment Council (SEAC) was given the power to 'keep under review all aspects of external qualifications' (Nisbet and Greig, 2007a: 53). The 1997 Education Act gave the Qualifications and Curriculum Authority (QCA) wider regulatory powers to accredit qualifications, that is, authorise awarding bodies to operate qualifications that met QCA's requirements. These regulatory powers were ceded to the Office of Qualifications and Examinations Regulation (Ofqual) in 2010.

Ofqual ensures public confidence in standards and regulates qualifications, **examinations** and tests in England by:

- monitoring and holding accountable the awarding bodies that offer and deliver qualifications
- ensuring that qualifications are fair and comparable with other qualifications
- monitoring standards in qualifications, examinations and assessments
- monitoring the quality of the marking of examinations and other assessments. (Ofqual, 2010a)

The principal regulatory tools that Ofqual uses in regulating tests and qualifications are codes of practice and qualifications and subject criteria. These are important when regulating high-stakes, high take-up assessments such as national curriculum tests, GCSEs and A levels, as well as when:

- an organisation has no track record of awarding regulated tests or qualifications
- an awarding body is recognised to offer a new type of qualification which would require new ways of working, or approaches to qualification design or assessment
- a new type of qualification or assessment is introduced that will be taken by large numbers of learners
- when there are concerns about qualifications offered by a particular awarding body. (Ofqual, 2010a)

Subject criteria set out the knowledge, understanding, skills and assessment objectives common to all specifications in that subject. They provide the framework within which awarding bodies create the syllabus details. Those specifications must also meet the common and qualifications criteria as defined in *The Statutory Regulation of External Qualifications in England, Wales and Northern Ireland* (QCA, 2004). Common criteria set out the functions of qualifications, content, assessment (including design of assessment and application of assessment methods) and determination and reporting of results (including aggregation and **grading**). Additional criteria for different types of qualification, including GCSEs and A levels, provide more detail on content, assessment and reporting.

The *National Curriculum Assessments: Code of Practice* (Ofqual, 2010c) and *National Curriculum Assessments Regulatory Framework* (Ofqual, 2009) govern all aspects of the assessment process, including common and subject criteria, test development, administration, marking, results data collection and reporting, and the monitoring system. The goal is to ensure testing agencies maintain standards and develop assessments that are fair and effective in measuring students' achievement. Assessments both for national curriculum tests and qualifications are judged against five criteria: **validity**; **reliability**; **comparability**; minimisation of bias; and manageability.

Criteria and codes of practice are intended to help ensure consistency and comparability of standards across testing agencies and awarding bodies, and that rigour is maintained. However, that rigour comes at a price; awarding bodies have less flexibility to innovate and teachers complain that they are losing professional control over what is taught and instead have to teach to tests and examinations (Baird and Lee-Kelley, 2009).

FURTHER READING

Boyle, A. (2008). *The Regulation of Examinations and Qualifications: An International Study*. Coventry: Ofqual.

Zajda, J. (2006). 'Introduction: decentralisation and privatisation in education – the role of the state'. In J. Zajda (ed.), *Decentralisation and Privatisation in Education: The Role of the State*. Amsterdam: Springer.

USEFUL WEBSITE

International Review of Curriculum and Assessment Frameworks Internet Archive (INCA). Available at: www.inca.org.uk

reliability

Reliability refers to the extent to which the scores produced by a test or results of an assessment are consistent, dependable and replicable. Reliability is a necessary but not sufficient condition of validity. It relates to those taking the assessment, those marking the assessment and to aspects of the assessment design itself.

Reliability is analogous to what scientists call 'replication'. A scientific experiment is regarded as reliable if it can be replicated giving the same results each time it is carried out. The extent to which an assessment task and process is deemed reliable is indicated by whether or not it would produce the same or very similar scores for the same students at different times in different places and regardless of who is marking the assessment. From the students' perspective, this is dependent on whether or not they can perform to the same level and standard under different conditions or at different times. From the assessor's perspective, it is dependent on whether different assessors make the same assessment decisions, or whether an individual assessor makes the same assessment decisions on different occasions and in different circumstances. Within the design of assessment itself, there is also a number of conditions to be met to ensure reliability.

RELIABILITY AS CONSISTENCY WITHIN THE TEST OR ASSESSMENT ITSELF

Within a test or an assessment that offers a choice of questions aimed at assessing the same aspects of knowledge or skills – technically called 'constructs' – the questions need to be designed in such a way that they produce the same scores if the assessment is to be deemed reliable. The same principle applies to two different assessments or tests (alternate form) aimed at assessing the same knowledge or skills both in terms of coverage and levels of difficulty. Reliability between different test items within tests and across different versions of assessments must be measured to ensure **comparability** of levels and standards of what is being tested across time (from one year to the next) and place (from one **awarding body** to another). An item can be a question, a problem to be solved, an exercise or any other aspect or unit of an assessment whose purpose is to elicit a response that can be scored separately as correct, incorrect or partially correct. The item must be designed to elicit from students indicators of the knowledge or skills that the assessment is measuring. An example of an item in a numeracy test would be a problem that requires the students to demonstrate that they understand how to subtract one number from another.

An assessment can be considered reliable if it provides a consistent set of measurements of whatever it is supposed to measure. Reliability requires not only that an individual mark, score or grade is accurate, but also that this mark, score or grade bears the appropriate relationship to

key concepts in educational assessment

any other in the same set of scores. A further condition of reliability in the types of assessments designed to identify low, average and high-achieving students is that the assessment requires questions or items that range from those the lowest achievers can answer correctly to those which only the highest achievers can answer well. The meaning of reliable here is that the assessment is able to fulfil one of its key purposes, which is to **discriminate** (sort or rank attainment) accurately between students.

MEASURES OF RELIABILITY

The reliability of items within an assessment or of an assessment by comparison with another or previous assessment can be measured by using a statistical procedure known as a correlation, meaning the extent to which two variables tend to appear together. In order to undertake this measure, the correlation is given a numerical value known as a coefficient. A reliability coefficient is measured from 0.0 to 1.0. A measure of 0.0 means that the assessment is not reliable at all, whereas a measure of 1.0 indicates perfect reliability. In reality, since there is error in any assessment, one cannot reach a reliability coefficient of 1.0. The following are generally agreed: 0.0 to 0.2 = no or very weak correlation; 0.2 to 0.4 = weak correlation; 0.4 to 0.7 = moderate correlation; 0.7 to 0.9 = strong correlation; 0.9 to 1.0 = very strong correlation. There are various methods deployed to demonstrate reliability. Each of these has its merits and limitations affecting the degree of reliability that can be claimed.

Test–retest

This is where the same assessment is given to the same students at different times. If both assessments generate the same or very similar scores then the assessment is deemed reliable. Error can arise if students recall the correct answers from the first assessment and improve their scores, and the organisation and administration of this process can be unwieldy and expensive.

Alternate form testing

This is where two different assessments designed to measure the same knowledge or skills are carried out with the same group of students. This reduces the error noted above occurring since students will not be able to recall the content of the second assessment and it is therefore likely to produce more reliable results. However, designing such assessments so that they are consistently equivalent is technically demanding.

Split halves

This measure offers an alternative and is where responses to items of an assessment taken by students at a single sitting are divided into two halves, say by separating all odd from all even numbered questions, with scores from each half correlated to determine reliability. However, the limitation here is that reliability is now compromised by applying only to each half of the assessment and not to the whole assessment. Normally, the longer the assessment the more reliable it is likely to be. Splitting the assessment into two halves in this way reduces its length, thereby also reducing reliability. To address this issue, statistical formulae have been developed such as Spearman Brown, to enable a further estimate to be made about the reliability of the whole assessment.

Internal consistency

Internal consistency can be measured by using other reliability coefficients such as Kuder-Richardson (KR 20). This can be applied to multiple-choice questions in particular, where individual answers are either right or wrong, and without having to split the assessment, or to measure the reliability of two items where a student has a choice of one question or another. A further coefficient, Cronbach's Alpha has been designed to be used with assessments where the responses required are not simply right or wrong but may be, for instance, on a rating scale. It is 'equivalent to all possible split-half reliability coefficients that could be created from the test but goes further' (Wright, 2007: 129). It enables one to estimate the reliability of different parts of the assessment, creating an opportunity for the removal of unreliable items and improvement of the assessment. These calculations are normally carried out using a software package such as SPSS or Excel, entering the scores of individuals for each item and applying the statistical formula. In this way, a reliability coefficient can be determined for all of the variables within a test or assessment.

RELIABILITY AND SOURCES OF ERROR AND BIAS RELATING TO SUBJECT, ASSESSMENT METHOD, ADMINISTRATION, CANDIDATES AND MARKERS OF ASSESSMENTS

A caveat to all of the above is that these measures of reliability apply more readily to subjects assessed via closed responses related to a fixed or points-based **mark scheme**. Where subjects are assessed using grade descriptors and criteria, a high level of reliability is harder to establish. This would apply to types of work subject to more open-ended assessment such as essays, creative work or **performance-based** tasks. This is truer the lower the level of **attainment** that is being assessed. The higher the level of education, the greater the parity of (un)reliability between all subjects requiring demonstration of abstract, evaluative or critical thinking since experts can disagree about what constitutes these characteristics in a specialist domain where new knowledge is being created and developed.

Administration issues affecting reliability include clarity and cultural bias in instruction to candidates, parity of support to students, physical conditions and distractions including time of day and year, and the recording of marks. Candidates themselves may perform unreliably at the moment of assessment due to variables including emotional and physical well-being. Performance could vary from occasion to occasion or from question to question or task to task on the same occasion.

INTER-RATER RELIABILITY AND RELIABILITY OVER TIME

Assessors can be affected consciously or unconsciously by assumed characteristics of the candidate including gender and ethnicity or school designation in relation to presumptions about attainment and performance (Gipps, 2012). They might be overly biased in favour of particular criteria such as good presentation or use of language, or harsher in the marking of a subject in which they have greater personal expertise.

However, the *Ofqual Code of Practice for Assessments in England, Wales and Northern Ireland* (Ofqual, 2011) states that the public interest in examinations extends to the proper maintenance of consistent standards over time in order for awards to have credibility and currency regardless of the year in which a candidate sits the assessment. Therefore, an assessment team must seek to ensure that a candidate scores the same mark, irrespective of who marks the work, in order to make the assessment **fair** and reliable. Marks awarded to all candidates by all assessors involved should form an internally consistent and accurate set of marks, as free from error as if one highly reliable marker had marked them all. All assessors are required to be scrupulous in their marking and to have their marking checked for clerical errors as well as for technical accuracy.

Assessment teams seek to ensure inter-rater reliability in a number of ways. Each time an assessment is set, this includes the use of the same assessment objectives, specification requirements and specification grids, and the use of straightforward, unambiguous mark schemes and weightings that can be interpreted consistently by all assessors, even though the content will vary from year to year. Also required is the **standardisation** of assessors at the outset of the marking period, the monitoring of assessors throughout the time that they are marking and **moderation** procedures. These can include the sampling of marking, 'blind', double or multiple marking. One possible problem with multiple marking is that of 'regression to the mean'. This occurs when assessors, wary of having their judgements questioned, play safe and award a middle-of-the-range mark in order to avoid controversy. It can also occur when a moderator or adjudicator splits the difference between varied marks. An alternative is to use 'pendulum moderation' where the adjudicator, faced with two widely different judgements, has to choose the higher or lower rather than taking an average.

THE RELATIONSHIP BETWEEN RELIABILITY AND VALIDITY

A test or an assessment can be reliable, always producing the same scores, without being **valid** in the same way that an inaccurate set of weighing scales may always give the same incorrect weight. But an assessment cannot be valid unless it is also reliable because to be valid it must accurately assess what it is designed to assess. Yet it is often considered that there is to some extent a trade-off between the two as features of an assessment. That is to say, by enhancing reliability you may reduce validity and vice versa. The *Life in the UK Test* for citizenship is a case in point as an example of assessment that produces reliable scores but whose validity is questionable. Take this question, for example (Dillon, 2007: 81):

Why did Protestant Huguenots from France come to Britain?

A. To escape famine
B. To escape religious persecution
C. To invade and seize land
D. To seek refuge from war

Assuming there is strong consensus among historians that the official answer is B then the authors of this question can claim 100% reliability.

However, whether it is valid, as an appropriate part of an assessment of a person's suitability to be a UK citizen, is very much open to debate. For the purposes of this particular assessment, a movement away from questions that assess the recall of facts, that may or may not be perceived to be relevant to citizenship, towards more discursive modes of assessment might improve content validity but could well reduce the consistency of scoring of answers because of assessor subjectivity. This would reduce reliability, which in turn reduces overall validity.

FURTHER READING

Brennan, R.L. (ed.). (2006). *Educational Measurement* (4th edn). Lanham, MD: Rowman & Littlefield.

Chartered Institute of Educational Assessors (CIEA) (2007). *Assessment reliability.* Available at: www.ciea.co.uk

Gipps, C. V. and Murphy, P. (1994). *A Fair Test?: Assessment, Achievement and Equity.* Buckingham: Open University Press.

Miller, D., Linn, R. L. and Gronlund, N. E. (2009). *Measurement and Assessment in Teaching.* (10th edn). Upper Saddle River, NJ: Pearson Education.

Opposs, D. and He, Q. (2012) *Ofqual's Reliability Compendium.* Coventry: Ofqual.

Standardisation

Standardisation is about ensuring that all assessors involved in marking the work of candidates do so consistently and accurately. It establishes a common standard of marking linked to the standard set for the work being assessed that helps maintain quality of marking both during the marking period and across a programme over time.

SETTING AND COMPARING STANDARDS

Wiliam (1996: 287) defines standard setting as 'the identification of certain points on a mark scale with particular performance standards, with the intention of enhancing the inferences that are warranted from the test scores'. The setting of standards guiding the scope and level of ability expected in the assessment of curriculum content requires expert consensus expressed in terms that enable comparability across time and across **awarding bodies**. It normally relates to high-stakes summative assessments where outcomes affect future education or employment opportunities for students. These are then made available at national level as statements about what students should be achieving at different stages or levels.

The obvious purpose of standardisation of scope and level and how this translates into assessment design is to 'avoid irrelevant factors that might distort comparison between individuals' (Koretz, 2008: 23). However, it nevertheless reflects subjective value judgements (Cresswell, 2001; Gardner *et al.*, 2010) about what is considered significant and desirable learning, behaviour or attitudes. Communication of the meaning of standards can be assisted with exemplification or model answers where appropriate, although this is also perceived to be problematic if it poses a constraint on, rather than an aid to, learning and development. The monitoring of the extent to which standards can be compared, between different awarding bodies for instance, involves the sampling of student scripts including those at grade boundaries using both statistical methods and expert judgement (see **comparability**). However, although the existence of these processes can offer reassurance about enhanced reliability and validity in standards setting and maintenance, neither method is considered superior and there is still no clear and agreed understanding ultimately of what the notion of 'same standard' actually represents (Newton *et al.*, 2007).

STANDARDISATION OF THE MARKING PROCESS

It is necessary for formal summative assessments to be standardised, that is, to be administered, fixed in their scope and level of difficulty and marked in a consistent way. This allows the assessment a measure of transparency and means that the outcomes of the assessment can be scrutinised and questioned. It is also common to introduce an appeals process if the outcome of the assessment affects the life chances of the individual.

Fundamental underpinning of the standardisation of the assessment process is provided by a **mark scheme**. This should ideally be written at the same time as the assessment although, until some of the actual responses of students are seen, a mark scheme is likely to have only provisional status. Although question-setters try to anticipate the likely responses to each of the assessment questions or tasks, it is usually the case that live scripts include responses that have not been anticipated, but that are worthy of credit. The mark scheme therefore usually undergoes a series of revisions, amplifications and refinements.

The complexity and administrative demands of the standardisation process vary according to the size of the candidate population (see **moderation**). In UK public examinations, where candidates can number many thousands, and assessment might be carried out by dozens of markers, the process is far more formal. It is likely to involve a physical or virtual standardisation meeting, not only for examinations that are marked through e-assessment online, but also for examination scripts marked by red pen in the traditional way. This should ensure all examiners share understandings and can reliably apply the mark scheme. Standardisation also entails assessors making judgements about the same work and then comparing their decisions to the prescribed standards and the candidate's performance in relation to those standards.

Following the standardisation meeting, the work of assistant examiners is monitored by team leaders through the sampling of scripts. Examiners are expected to work to a pre-determined tolerance, or allowable margin of error, which might be established for each individual question, or for an answer script as a whole. Inconsistent markers whose judgements are considered erratic might be stopped from marking and have their work re-marked. If markers are found to be consistently harsh or severe, then their marks might be corrected by use of a downward or upwards adjustment. Some awarding bodies use quite sophisticated algorithms to determine adjustment factors by statistical means.

FURTHER READING

Newton, P., Baird, J. A., Goldstein, H., Patrick, H. and Tymms, P. (eds) (2007). *Techniques for Monitoring the Comparability of Examination Standards*. London: QCA.

Ofqual (2011). GCSE, GCE, *Principal Learning and Project Code of Practice*. Coventry: Ofqual.

Supply-type assessments include short-answer, essay and data-response items, where the assessor provides a task to which the candidate supplies a written response. They tend to be open-ended, in contrast to selection-type assessments, which include multiple-choice, matching and true/false items, which are closed rather than open-ended, and the candidate selects the correct or 'best' answer.

The distinction between supply and selection is often discussed in the context of objectivity, an issue that is related to the **reliability** of an assessment. Objectivity means that there is an absence of inconsistency in marking and grading, arising from subjective judgements or inadvertent bias on the part of the question-setter or marker.

SUPPLY-TYPE QUESTIONS

There is a hierarchy among supply-type items in which short-answer items can assess knowledge, computation and skill; restricted essays can assess knowledge, understanding, application and analysis; and extended essays can assess understanding, application, analysis, evaluation and creation (Gronlund and Waugh, 2009). Short-answer items should only have one answer and restricted essays need to contain scaffolding that helps candidates shape their response.

Extended essay questions are popular among assessors because they are relatively quick and easy to write, provide opportunities for a creative and, to some extent, open-ended response, and can test the student's ability to put together a logical chain of argument. They are therefore believed to be a good method of testing higher-level cognitive skills. On the other hand, if the answer to an essay merely recalls a narrative remembered from class, or regurgitated from notes, the cognitive performance can actually be at a very low level. A factor to take into consideration is that the marking and grading of extended answer questions can be very expensive and time-consuming to complete.

Using supply-type assessment, it is nearly impossible to prevent an assessor's own preconceptions affecting the mark achieved by a candidate. These preconceptions can arise from the assessor's knowledge and experience in the subject area, writing style and a whole array of linguistic and cultural factors, thereby introducing an element of unintended bias into the question. This can also arise in a large marking team due to different members working to different interpretations of the criteria, or having different opinions about academic standards. It can also arise due to differing degrees of experience and competence among examiners. The assessors' skills then lie in designing a **mark scheme,** and organising **standardisation** and **moderation** processes that reward at an appropriate level and ensure consistency within acceptable tolerances. Appropriate training for assessors is crucial to ensure the reliability of this type of item.

SELECTION-TYPE QUESTIONS

Because it is assumed that selection-type test questions, such as true/false, matching or multiple-choice, are much easier than supply-type to mark and grade objectively, assessments that contain them are sometimes referred to as 'objective tests'.

The stem of a multiple-choice item is the introductory part of the item that sets the scene, or posits a scenario, and poses a problem or makes a statement that requires a response. There will then follow, typically, four or five options. One of these will be the key or correct or best answer. The others will be distractors, which must be skilfully written so that they appear plausible to the badly-prepared student, but that nevertheless do not undermine the unique correctness of the key, which must be water-tight. It is important that the correct option does not contain clues to the answer, such as containing similar words to those found in the stem, using a different style of language from the distractors, or providing greater detail than the other choices.

True/false type questions can be used instead of multiple-choice items where more than one answer is possible. They should be short, simple and clear, as in the following example:

A basic principle of physics is that energy can neither be created nor be destroyed. True or False?

This could, of course, be turned into a multiple-choice question by expressing it in the following way:

A basic principle of physics is that energy:

A. can be created but not destroyed
B. can be destroyed but not created
C. can be destroyed and created
D. can be neither destroyed nor created.

Matching-type items are also common and can be used where the material is homogenous. Good practice in creating this type of item is to use either a smaller or larger number of possible answers than the original match words, so that a candidate does not automatically get some right (or wrong) because he or she got others right.

A superficial attraction of selection-type assessments to institutions and **awarding bodies** is that they are cheap to administer. This might be true for tests of poor quality, but quality assurance is anything but cheap, involving the hiring of highly-experienced question-setters and the use of pre-tests to iron out any undetected flaws in the items. A major advantage is that once developed and pre-tested satisfactorily, assessments can be held in an item bank. Statistics for facility (difficulty) and **discrimination** can be built up over time, and tests can therefore be compiled to order, by using the assessments in the item bank and can be predicted reasonably accurately to perform within certain parameters.

There are alleged disadvantages to selection-type assessments. For example, they encourage guessing. As Wood, R. (1991: 32) maintains, however, 'No assessment technique has been rubbished quite like multiple choice, unless it be graphology.' Nevertheless, as Wiliam (2008) explains, multiple-choice questions can be used to assess high-order skills and understanding.

To avoid the criticism of 'guessing', four or five option items may be preferable to true/false items. Provided that bias and subjectivity are edited out at the setting stage, selection-type items easily out-perform supply-type items in terms of objectivity at the marking stage, since they can be marked by machines rather than human beings. However, while some psychometric experts, especially in the USA, might well dispute this, it is generally accepted in the UK that human markers and supply-type questions are required for high-risk assessments that seek to test complex concepts and higher-order skills.

Downing, S. and Haladyna, T.M. (eds) (2006). *Handbook of Test Development*. Mahwah, NJ: Lawrence Erlbaum Associates.

Haladyna, T. M. (2004). *Developing and Validating Multiple-Choice Test Items* (3rd edn) London: Routledge.

Hunt, G. H. and Touzel, T. J. (2009). *Effective Teaching: Preparation and Implementation* (4th edn) Springfield, IL: Charles C. Thomas Publications.

Wiliam, D. (2008). 'Six degrees of integration: an agenda for joined up assessment'. In *Documents of Proceedings*, Chartered Institute of Educational Assessors (CIEA), conference, London. Available at: http://www.ciea.co.uk

Validity refers to accuracy in assessment design – the extent to which any assessment measures what it has been designed to measure. It also refers to the interpretation of results of an assessment – the extent to which certain inferences can be made from an assessment's outcomes.

Validity

An essential quality\ of an assessment is the extent to which it is valid, that is, that the assessment measures the content, skills and understanding that it sets out to measure in such a way that accurate and fair conclusions about performance can be drawn from its outcomes. According to Messick's (1989: 13) classic definition, validity is a multi-faceted but unitary concept: 'Validity is an integrated evaluative judgement of the degree to which empirical evidence and theoretical rationales support the *adequacy* and *appropriateness* of *inferences* and *actions* based on the test scores or other modes of assessment.' This definition takes into account not only conclusions that can be drawn, but the end results of those conclusions.

135

The 1999 Standards for Educational and Psychological Testing went on to define validity as 'the degree to which evidence and theory support the interpretation of test scores entailed by proposed uses of tests ... the process of validation involves accumulating evidence to provide a sound scientific basis for the proposed score interpretations' (AERA, APA and NCME, 1999: 9). Moss *et al.*, (2006: 109) stress the importance of validity theory, stating that it 'provides guidance about what it means to say that an interpretation, decision or action is more or less sound; about the sorts of evidence, reasoning and criteria by which soundness might be judged; and about how to develop more sound interpretations, decisions and actions'.

It is generally held that a necessary, though not sufficient, condition of validity is **reliability** – the extent to which you can get consistent results across many assessment attempts. Wright (2007: 145) offers a further three essential conditions of validity: 'the fidelity of test items to the construct or curriculum being measured, the linkage between the test and independent indicators of the construct or curriculum being measured and the appropriateness of the use made of the test scores'.

Suppose, for example, a person is being assessed in order to qualify as a crane driver. Bearing in mind the content being assessed, whether that content reflects the attributes or qualities – otherwise known as the construct – that comprise crane driving and the judgements that will be made on the assessment outcomes, should this assessment take the form of:

(a) a practical test of psychomotor skills using a real crane
(b) multiple-choice style questions on the step-by-step manoeuvres required to manipulate the crane's controls, or
(c) an essay entitled 'How I would use a crane to lift and move a load from one position to another'?

The most logical is answer a, in terms of the fidelity of the item to the construct, although it may not necessarily be the most viable. Method a, for instance, requires access to a real crane, and is likely to have higher costs in terms of time and money than the other two. Method b could, perhaps, be linked to a computer simulation, which would have cost implications during the development phase, but lower operating costs than a real crane, with the possibility of online access at a distance once in use. Method c might well be regarded as the most attractive type of assessment on purely cost grounds, and it could well be quite a reliable assessment, in terms of consistency of results. However, it is arguable whether it is as valid an assessment as either of the other two. There would need to be careful consideration of the possibility that candidates are being assessed on their ability to write an essay about driving a crane, rather than their ability to drive a crane.

Another consideration relates to manageability. The extent to which assessment design is deemed manageable depends upon on resources, including cost and time, available to those being assessed and those assessing them. In the crane-driving example the cheapest and potentially most manageable approach is c. Setting an essay question requires no finely-calibrated multiple-choice question item piloting, and no expensive equipment, but if chosen it clearly demonstrates that manageability can weaken validity.

FACETS OF VALIDITY

The considerations most commonly taken into account when judging if an assessment can be used in a valid way are:

Face validity

Does the assessment look as if it is assessing what it is supposed to be assessing? In the example above, it would be argued that for face validity an assessment of crane driving and operating skills should be taken on a crane.

Content validity

Does the assessment adequately cover the topics contained in a curriculum, programme of study or syllabus and focus on the most important parts? The assessed elements should represent, as much as is feasible, the entire range of possible content. To use the same example, should the crane driver pass the qualifying assessment by answering questions on, or demonstrating competence in lifting and moving loads while not being confronted with questions or demonstrations on how to reverse safely?

Construct validity

Does the assessment adequately reflect the appropriate constructs within the curriculum, programme of study or syllabus? That is to say, important concepts, attributes, qualities or traits, such as mathematical reasoning, reading comprehension, intelligence or creativity are adequately covered. If not, we have something that measurement experts call construct under-representation. An example would be the extent to which a language comprehension assessment can be deemed to assess the entire range of reading skills. A different potential problem is construct irrelevance. An example would be long-winded and complex word problems in a mathematics assessment, which might lead good mathematicians to get the answer wrong. Expert assessment developers pay careful attention to avoid construct under-representation and construct irrelevance. In the case of the crane driver, not to assess gear-handling skills would constitute construct under-representation while assessing high-level verbal skills would constitute construct irrelevance.

Predictive validity

Does the assessment successfully identify those who will succeed in future related endeavours and those who will not? This is notoriously difficult to determine in advance and understandably contentious in high-stakes assessments. UK university admissions tutors, for instance, place great emphasis on A level grades, on the assumption that they are good predictors of performance at degree level. It is difficult to verify whether this assumption is valid, because of the practical difficulties of comparing the subsequent educational trajectory of those who are selected with those who are rejected. Predictive validity is also concerned with whether one assessment can predict the outcomes of another. For example, can a 'mock' final assessment predict the outcomes of the final assessment itself? Can success in an assessment at the age of 16 predict the outcomes of a final assessment at 18 in a different, or even the same domain? Does manipulating a crane under controlled testing conditions mean that someone will be a good crane operator once hired?

Consequential (backwash) validity

This relates to how assessment results are used. Are they used for formative or summative purposes, for instance, and what sort of **feedback** is given to the candidate? What is the impact on participants arising from the assessment process, interpretations and decisions? To what extent do the results affect public perceptions? How valid is it to declare a school or college *per se* highly successful when its students achieve excellent results? Do the results affect policy either within an educational institution, or at governmental level? What are the educational consequences of assessment, in terms of their impact on learning and teaching, and ultimately what are their economic and social consequences? How valid, for example, was the assumption that was made in England and Wales from the 1940s to at least the 1960s that children could appropriately be segregated into different types of educational experience on the basis of a series of literacy, numeracy, general knowledge and IQ tests at the age of 11? How valid is the widely-held assumption that there is some sort of divide between 'academic' and 'vocational' learning, teaching and assessment? Some people in the field of educational assessment see consequential validity as different from the other facets (see Kane, 2001; Koretz, 2008; Moss *et al.*, 2006) because, while important, it is difficult to associate it directly with the assessment itself.

VALIDITY, FAIRNESS AND BIAS

The validity of an assessment can be equated to its **fairness** (Gipps and Murphy, 1994). In turn, fairness can be closely linked to the avoidance of bias in assessment (Cole and Moss, 1989; Smith, 1998; Stobart *et al.*, 1992). Bias can act as a source of invalidity if, for example, an assessor makes incorrect assumptions about the linguistic ability of candidates, as in the example above of an assessment aimed at assessing numeracy but that contained 'wordy' problem-style questions that students could answer if they were expressed using mathematical symbols instead of verbally. Similarly, questions can be biased if they make assumptions about the age, sex, race or general culture of the population who make up the candidature. Stobart (2005) points out that one sex often outperforms the other when assessments are framed in certain contexts. For example, boys do better than girls on questions that relate to science, technical matters, war and diplomacy, while girls perform better than boys when questions concern humanities or human relationships. He argues that for assessment systems to be both valid and fair, they should include a variety of modes, contexts and tasks.

MINIMISING THREATS TO VALIDITY

Crooks *et al.* (1996) depicted assessment as a linked chain comprising administration, scoring, aggregation, generalisation, extrapolation, evaluation, decision and impact, and analysed threats to validity that could be associated with each link. Some of the threats are difficult to curtail, for example students' anxiety or lack of motivation, but others can be minimised through careful attention to task development, scoring and marker training. For example, one way of improving validity and therefore minimising invalidity in assessment is for assessors to ensure that assessments are accompanied by carefully constructed **mark schemes,** which are closely linked to the assessment criteria published for the curriculum in question, and which are implemented by well-prepared and coordinated teams of markers.

MEASURING VALIDITY

We can measure validity in a variety of ways. Many of these are in fact measures of reliability, an essential condition of validity. They include analysis of the assessment's content, statistical analysis of people's performance on an assessment, statistical comparisons between performance on an assessment with performance on another assessment, and/ or students' own responses to an assessment. Most of these measures involve what is known as correlation – the positive or negative relationship between one set of factors or variables and another. For example, we could compare predicted scores from a 'mock' examination with the actual scores in a final examination and check the extent to which they produce the same results. Where they do, we say they are strongly correlated and statistical procedures have been developed to measure this relationship.

Correlating the extent to which the 'mock' assessment predicted the outcomes of the final assessment would give us something known as a validity coefficient. We can also determine the validity coefficient by analysing the items within an assessment and comparing the marks gained for each item with each other. This will give us a construct validity measure. These correlations generate numbers between −1.00 (perfectly negatively correlated, i.e. the mock *never* predicts the final) and +1.00 (perfectly positively correlated, i.e. the mock *always* predicts the final). A correlation of 0.0 would mean that the two variables being measured bear no relationship to each other. The aim is to get a number as close to 1.0 as possible.

Analyses are usually done by entering scores into an SPSS (statistical package for social sciences) software programme or Excel and using the functionality to find the correlations between the items on an assessment. Often, Cronbach's Alpha, which is a measure of internal consistency or reliability within an assessment, is used to determine the levels of reliability for each item and the subsequent validity coefficient. Usually a validity coefficient of at least 0.6 is considered adequate in any assessment. Since validity is relative, that is, related to a particular assessment, taken by a particular group at a particular time, dependence on the validity coefficient alone is not considered sufficient to deem the assessment valid. It must be taken into account alongside concerns about content, construct and consequential validity so that we balance the demands of accuracy with those of interpretation and inference.

FURTHER READING

Brennan, R. L. (ed.) (2006). *Educational Measurement* (4th edn). Lanham, MD: Rowman & Littlefield.

Crooks, T., Kane, M. and Cohen, A. (1996). 'Threats to the valid use of assessments'. *Assessment in Education: Principles, Policies and Practice*, 3 (3), 265–85.

Kane, M. (2001). 'Current concerns in validity theory'. *Journal of Educational Measurement*, 38 (4), 319–42.

Moss, P., Girard, B. and Haniford, L. (2006). 'Validity in educational assessment'. *Review of Research in Education*, 30, 109–62.

Tanner, H. and Jones, S. (2003). *Marking and Assessment* (2nd edn). London: Continuum.

Wiliam, D. (1992). 'Some technical issues in assessment: a user's guide'. *British Journal for Curriculum and Assessment*, 2 (3), 11–20.

.... Vocational Assessment ....

Vocational assessment relates to the assessment of vocational education and training (VET). Traditionally this prepared trainees for jobs in specific trades or occupations, and is an assessment system that concentrates on the qualifications that recognise skills related to a particular workplace or vocational area.

Vocational assessment is applied in a variety of contexts ranging from school to work. It also applies to occupational tools and processes that support clients with special educational needs and disabilities. Debra Perry (2011: 1) defines vocational assessment as 'the process of determining an individual's interests, abilities and aptitudes and skills to identify vocational strengths, needs and career potential. Vocational assessment may use a variety of standardized techniques (e.g. tests) or non-standardized approaches (e.g. interviews, observing people). Vocational assessment is part of the vocational guidance process and usually results in recommendations for training and employment'.

Vocational assessment is aimed primarily at students in the later stages of education, young adults or those with special needs and is a way of introducing them to the world of work. Typically, it assesses the skills and aptitudes needed to function in the workplace. Often this type of assessment integrates with apprenticeship schemes. Vocational education and assessment in the UK developed through the 20th century largely independent of the state. However, in 1944 the Education Act recognised the importance of vocational education and assessment and set up a tripartite system of grammar schools, secondary modern schools and secondary technical schools where the focus was on vocational education and assessment.

Within the vocational system, there is a different assessment regime from the more recognisable examination system. Typically, this is based upon a detailed specification that states the purpose and aim of the assessment. It is common for assessment methods to be detailed in this specification. For example, assessments may include evidence based upon practical demonstrations of competence, observations by individual assessors or assessment teams, the completion of complex tasks over a significant amount of time, witness statements, presentations, group activities, **oral assessment**, simulations, tests of skills, assignments, projects, case studies, as well as the recognition of any prior learning. The specification then details the learning outcomes (what the learner will do), the assessment criteria (a description of what the learner can do) and exemplifications or some indication of evidence that may be used to determine whether the assessment criteria have been fulfilled. The candidate completes the work, based on the specification and the assessment criteria that accompany it.

This is then assessed internally by an assessor, who needs to be prequalified in order to assess. His or her judgements then need to be overseen by the internal verifier (IV) who submits the assessment data and an audit trail to an external verifier (EV) from the awarding organisation, who verifies (or otherwise) the authenticity of the procedures that have been undertaken and checks the evidence in order to maintain independent rigour. There must be valid, authentic and sufficient evidence for all of the assessment criteria. Holistic assessment is encouraged and one piece of evidence may be used to meet the evidence requirements of more than one learning outcome or assessment criterion.

A vocational assessment can be characterised in a similar way to **work-based assessment**. There are specifications that set out the details of assessment in the following formats:

1 An emphasis on outcomes, usually multiple outcomes, each one distinctive and considered separately
2 The belief that these outcomes can and should be specified to the point where they are 'transparent', so that assessors, candidates and interested third parties (potential employers or end-users) understand what is being assessed and what has been achieved
3 The de-coupling of assessment from particular institutions or learning programmes (Wolf, 2001).

Since the 1970s, successive British governments have tried to expand VET with its associated assessment system, since labour markets have demanded increasing levels of skill and have become more specialised. This has been replicated in many western democracies. The range of assessments now extends beyond traditional practical skills in such areas as car mechanics, to include retail, hairdressing, tourism, information technology, engineering and manufacturing.

England has a strong tradition of vocationally related qualifications, both nationally specified – for example, General National Vocational Qualifications (GNVQ), applied GCSEs and A levels and the Diploma qualifications – and proprietary – for example, BTEC Firsts and Nationals. National programmes were developed because of perceived deficiencies in vocational education and training and each offered a government-supported, full-time programme for 14- to 19-year-olds. They fill what Hodgson and Spours (Hodgson and Spours, 2007; Nuffield Review, 2007) characterise as the middle track, that is, situated between academic and occupational routes, and are meant to attract students who are not yet ready to join the workforce, but are not enamoured of more traditional offerings. These qualifications are largely internally assessed. A recent review (Wolf, 2011) has questioned the usefulness of vocationally-related qualifications for 14- to 16-year-olds and the current government is taking measures to curtail their use for that age group.

However, in the USA, vocational assessment is sometimes viewed differently with strong links to vocational evaluation. This is a process where those students with physical impairments or learning difficulties, both specific and non-specific, learn about the functional impact of their impairment on their career options. They also learn about ways of overcoming any barriers to employment by the use of technologies. The process encourages an individual's involvement in his or her career and encourages individuals to make decisions for themselves.

In contrast, vocational assessment is seen in the UK as part and parcel of the more general vocational education and training (VET) system. This is linked to a wide range of vocational qualifications covering all occupational sectors through National Vocational Qualifications (NVQs). Wolf (2001) argues against the over-reliance on specified outcomes linked to criterion-referenced tests. This approach towards vocational assessment has manifested in the design of UK NVQs linked to allegedly uniform national occupational standards and skills testing as the basis for measuring work-related competence and capability, suggesting a common link between the purpose of VET systems for delivering work-based learning and work-based assessment as a means for delivering employability skills. In the UK, the post-compulsory education and training sector is now often referred to as the lifelong learning sector and links work-based learning to systems of work-based assessment.

Gonczi (2004) argues that it is reasonable to make the assumption that professional practice is essentially linked to the acquisition of professional competence and that work-based learning and integrated assessment systems form a powerful foundation and curriculum design for much of vocational education and training. This view of vocational assessment also links to the concept of accredited continuing professional development. Gardner and Coombs (2009) argue that it is possible to 'professionalise the professions' through vocational assessment in the workplace and that this can be validated as vocationally accredited and assessed forms of higher education and training.

Although the titles assessor, internal verifier and external verifier are not always used, for example in South Africa, the same procedure as that outlined above is followed in most contexts (DHETSA, 2012). In South Africa, a detailed system of vocational assessment has evolved, underpinned by a National Qualification Framework (NQF). Each specification sets out the purpose of the assessment and how it fits into the NQF. Its objectives are to:

- create an integrated national framework for learning achievements
- facilitate access to and progression within education, training and career paths
- enhance the quality of education and training
- redress unfair discrimination and past imbalances and thereby accelerate employment opportunities
- contribute to the holistic development of the student by addressing:
  - social adjustment and responsibility
  - moral accountability and ethical work orientation
  - economic participation
  - and nation building.

The last point about nation building highlights the purpose behind this system, which is very different from that found in the USA or UK. Here we see a nation trying to rebuild itself through a carefully thought-out system of vocational education and assessment. The principles that underpin these objectives are also confirmed within this nation-building concept:

- integration – to adopt a unified approach to education and training
- relevance – to be dynamic and responsive to national development needs
- coherence – to work within a consistent framework of principles and certification
- flexibility – to allow for creativity and resourcefulness when achieving learning outcomes
- participation – to enable stakeholders to participate in setting the assessment and the assessment criteria
- access – to address barriers to learning at each level to facilitate students' progress

- progression – to ensure that the qualification framework permits individuals to move through the levels of the national qualification
- portability – to enable students to transfer credits of qualifications from one learning institution to another
- articulation – to allow for vertical and horizontal mobility in the education system
- recognition of prior learning – to grant credits for a unit of learning following an assessment or if a student possesses the capabilities specified in the outcomes statement
- validity of assessment – to ensure assessment covers a broad range of knowledge, skills, values and attitudes (KSVAs) needed to demonstrate applied competency
- reliability – to assure assessment practices are consistent so that the same result or judgement is arrived at if the assessment is replicated in the same context
- fairness and transparency – to verify that no assessment process or method(s) hinders or unfairly advantages any student
- practicability and cost-effectiveness – to integrate assessment practices within an outcomes-based education and training system and strive for cost- and time-effective assessment. (DHETSA, 2012)

Vocational assessment has moved a long way over the last century. Beginning with trades schools set up in the UK in the early part of the 20th century where skills were taught independently of the state and assessed independently, to the system highlighted above, we see the change from independence to state prescription of national occupational standards. We also see the state prescribing not only the standards, but the methodology involved in assessment.

FURTHER READING

Gonczi, A. (2004). 'The new professional and vocational education'. In G. Foley (ed.), *Dimensions of Adult Learning: Adult Education and Training in a Global Era.* Maidenhead: Open University Press.

Wolf, A. (2001). *Competence-based assessment.* Available at: http://www.heacademy. ac.uk/assets/documents/resources/heca/heca_cl25.pdf

Wolf, A. (2011). *Review of Vocational Education – The Wolf Report.* London: Department for Education.

Work-based Assessment

> Work-based assessment relates to the assessment of competence at performing a certain task in the workplace, whatever the context may be. It is usually related to continuous professional development (CPD) but can in certain schemes offer credits at Higher Education Institutions (HEIs) that can be accumulated and cashed in for a qualification.

In order to develop a more effective workforce, work-based assessment was gradually introduced into Britain in the late 1980s. Since then the number of work-based assessments has mushroomed and transformed **vocational assessment**. The dominant assessment methodology tends to be competence-based or a skills-based derivative.

Work-based assessment is intrinsically linked to the conceptual framework of work-based learning and the need for people to develop a diverse range of skills and talents through on-the-job education and training. Historically, the ancient professions formed their own guilds and internal training systems linked to apprenticeships.

Although apprenticeships are still available, the trend today is for professionals such as those who practise medicine, architecture and law to embark upon work-based learning and assessment. Such courses are designed specifically to meet the needs of the sector where they take place and are typified by broad-based objectives that cut across traditional subject and sector domains and are precisely articulated. They generally consist of three main elements:

- A description of the competence being assessed (the learning outcome)
- A range statement that specifies the context and the conditions in which the competence has to be developed and displayed

- A set of criteria that describes how evidence can be gathered and recorded to display the competence.

The assessment of competences is always criterion-referenced; there are rarely any marks or grades awarded, rather a candidate is marked as competent or not yet competent, although some courses distinguish between basic competence, merit and distinction for those performing the competence at the highest level. To be successful, a candidate must display all of the performance criteria for that competence being assessed. In circumstances that offer nationally accredited qualifications, a rigorous **quality assurance** regime is expected to be put in place. Within the institution offering the award there needs to be an agreed system of checking the assessments (**internal verification**) where the outcomes and decisions about performance are moderated across the institution by a qualified assessor (internal verifier). An external verifier appointed by the awarding organisation checks and validates that the expected standards are being met.

The history of apprenticeships goes back to the Middle Ages with the concept being both recognised and applied internationally and embedded within frameworks of government apprenticeship schemes. Fuller and Unwin (1998: 154) argue for a reconceptualisation of apprenticeship schemes and claim that work-based learning and associated systems of assessment need to be more widely recognised as a legitimate form of learning over and above that which occurs in educational institutions and maintain that 'apprenticeship [is] a meaningful vehicle for the development and transference of occupational skills, knowledge and understanding (and that) work-based learning should be recognised as a transforming as well as functional process'.

Making this shift, from a *low-skills* transmissive teaching style to a more contextualised and cognitively higher-order practitioner-based approach to work-based learning and assessment, is something that has taken place only recently. This conceptual framework is then extended to professional practice models of workplace learning through ideas such as the development of the reflective practitioner (Schön, 1983). Such a conceptual framework sees work-based learning as part of a continuum of lifelong learning moving from the early stages of apprenticeship in, say, car maintenance, to advanced professional practitioners in, say, medicine. It therefore covers a broad curriculum of potential vocational assessments, potentially ranging from Levels 1 to 8 as defined and described by the European Qualifications Framework (EQF) to enable benchmarking of common standards and transnational workforce mobility (European Union, 2008).

Systems of work-based assessment therefore reflect the learning needs of the setting, which can range from simple tests and **coursework** related to vocational training objectives, through to action research projects linked to performance and change management goals within large institutions. Advanced systems of work-based assessment can link critical and creative thinking applied to targets aimed at changing workplace practices. They usually engage participants in learning activities designed to develop transferable skills to enable practice-based problem solving. Such an approach represents a radical model of work-based vocational education and training (VET) and continuing professional development (CPD) – one that is promoted by Gardner and Coombs (2009: 130) who maintain that the nature of action research projects stimulates activities within the workplace, thereby improving practice amongst practitioners. They also argue that the generic nature of action research means that professionals engaged in Masters-level programmes can effectively share projects across divergent professional boundaries.

Within the context of the medical profession, Norcini (2003) builds upon Miller's (1990) framework for assessing clinical competence. He argues that action in the workplace is built upon prior learning and knowledge and claims that work-based assessment is superior because it focuses on actual practice rather than artificial situations.

Despite these claims, many critics argue that such assessment regimes are overloaded with the bureaucracy needed to verify the competency, and many such assessments have become discredited through the need to collect and amass evidence.

FURTHER READING

Epstein, R. M. and Hundert, E. M. (2002). 'Defining and assessing professional competence'. *JAMA: The Journal of the American Medical Association*, 287 (2), 226–35.
Fuller, A. and Unwin, L. (2011). 'Apprenticeship as an evolving model of learning'. *Journal of Vocational Education and Training*, 63 (3), 261–6.

work-based assessment

references

AERA, APA and NCME (1999). *Standards for Educational and Psychological Testing.* Washington, DC: AERA.

AIAA (2007). *Recording and tracking pupils' attainment and progress: the use of assessment evidence at the time of inspection.* Available at: http://www.aaia.org.uk/pdf/publications

Assessment Reform Group (2002). *Assessment for Learning: 10 principles. Research-based principles to guide classroom practice.* Available at: http://arrts.gtcni.org.uk/gtcni/bitstream/2428/4623/1/Assessment%20for%20Learning%20-%2010%20principles.pdf

Assessment Reform Group (2006). *The Role of Teachers in the Assessment of Learning.* Cambridge: Cambridge University, Faculty of Education.

Au, W. (2009). *Unequal by Design: High-Stakes Testing and the Standardization of Inequality.* Abingdon: Routledge.

Baird, J.-A. (2007). 'Alternate conceptions of comparability'. In P. Newton, J. A. Baird, H. Goldstein, H. Patrick and P. Tymms (eds), *Techniques for Monitoring the Comparability of Examination Standards.* London: QCA.

Baird, J.-A. and Lee-Kelley, L. (2009). 'The dearth of managerialism in implementation of national examinations policy'. *Journal of Education Policy,* 24 (1), 55–81.

Baker, E. L. and Linn, R. L. (2002). *Validity Issues for Accountability Systems.* Los Angeles, CA: CSE Technical Report 585. CRESST.

Barker, I. (2010). 'Don't worry, be APPy'. *TES,* 14 May. Available at: http://www.tes.co.uk/article.aspx?storycode=6043711

BBC (2007). *England falls in reading league.* Available at: http://news.bbc.co.uk/1/hi/education/7117230.stm

BBC (2008a). *England's pupils in global top 10.* Available at: http://news.bbc.co.uk/1/hi/education/7773081.stm

BBC (2008b). *Big jump in top GCSE exam grades.* BBC News, 21 August. Available at: http://news.bbc.co.uk/1/hi/education/7574073.stm

BBC (2010). *UK schools fall in global ranking.* Available at: http://www.bbc.co.uk/news/education-11929277

Bennett, R. E. (1998). *Reinventing Assessment: Speculations on the Future of Large-Scale Educational Testing,* Princeton, NJ: ETS.

Bennett, R.E. (2011). 'Formative assessment: a critical review'. *Assessment in Education: Principles, Policy & Practice,* 18 (1), 5–25.

Bew Review (2011). *Independent review of Key Stage 2 testing, assessment and accountability. Final report.* Available at: http://www.education.gov.uk/ks2review

Black, P. (1998). *Testing, Friend or Foe?: The Theory and Practice of Assessment and Testing.* London: Falmer Press.

Black, P. and Wiliam, D. (1998a). 'Assessment and classroom learning'. *Assessment in Education: Principles, Policy & Practice,* 5 (1), 7–74.

Black, P. and Wiliam, D. (1998b). *Inside the Black Box: Raising Standards through Classroom Assessment.* Slough: NFER-Nelson.

Black, P., Harrison, C., Lee, C., Marshall, B. and Wiliam, D. (2003). *Assessment for Learning: Putting it into Practice.* Maidenhead: Open University Press.

Black, P., Harrison, C., Lee, C., Marshall, B. and Wiliam, D. (2004). *Working Inside the Black Box: Assessment for Learning in the Classroom.* Slough: NFER Nelson.

Bond, T. G. and Fox, C. M. (2001). *Applying the Rasch Model: Fundamental Measurement in the Human Sciences.* Mahwah, NJ: Lawrence Erlbaum Associates.

Boston, K. (2005). *Strategy, technology and assessment.* Keynote speech, 10th Annual Assessment Round Table. Melbourne, Australia.

Boud, D. (1988). *Developing Student Autonomy in Learning.* London: Kogan Page.

Boud, D., Cohen, R. and Sampson, J. (1999). 'Peer learning and assessment'. *Assessment & Evaluation in Higher Education,* 24 (4), 413–26.

Boud, D., Cohen, R. and Sampson, J. (eds) (2001). *Peer Learning in Higher Education: Learning from and with Each Other.* London: Kogan Page.

Boyle, A. (2008). *The regulation of examinations and qualifications: An international study.* Available at: http://www.inca.org.uk/ofqual-08-3736_regulation_of_examinations_and_qualifications.pdf

Boyle, A. and Hutchison, D. (2009). 'Sophisticated tasks in E-assessment: what are they and what are their benefits?'. *Assessment & Evaluation in Higher Education,* 34 (3), 305–19.

Broadfoot, P. (1999). *Empowerment or performativity? English assessment policy in the late twentieth century.* Paper presented at the Assessment Reform Group Symposium on Assessment Policy at the British Educational Research Association Annual Conference. Brighton, University of Sussex.

Broadfoot, P. (2007). *An Introduction to Assessment.* London: Continuum.

Chapman, D. W. and Snyder Jr, C. W. (2000). 'Can high-stakes national testing improve instruction? Reexamining conventional wisdom'. *International Journal of Educational Development,* 20 (6), 457–74.

Chartered Institute of Educational Assessors (CIEA) (2007). *Oral Language Modifier.* Available at: http://www.ciea.co.uk

Chartered Institute of Educational Assessors (CIEA) (2009). *CIEA Professional Framework.* Available at: http://www.ciea.co.uk

Clarke, S. (2005). *Formative Assessment in the Secondary Classroom.* London: Hodder & Stoughton.

Coaley, K. (2010). *An Introduction to Psychological Assessment and Psychometrics.* London: Sage.

Coe, R. (2010). 'Understanding comparability of examination standards'. *Research Papers in Education,* 25 (3), 271–84.

Coldron, J., Willis, B. and Wolstenholme, C. (2009). 'Selection by attainment and aptitude in English secondary schools'. *British Journal of Educational Studies,* 57 (3), 245–64.

Cole, N. and Moss, P. (1989). 'Bias in test use'. In R. L. Linn (ed.), *Educational Measurement* (3rd edn). New York: MacMillan.

Coombs, S. (2010). *Critical thinking, portfolio assessment and e-scaffolding of continuing professional development for knowledge elicitation*, AACE Global Learn International Conference. Penang, Malaysia.

Coombs, S. and McKenna, C. (2009). *Assessment for Learning: Concepts and reality*, IPDA Conference. Liverpool, UK.

Cresswell, M. J. (1996). 'Defining, setting and maintaining standards in curriculum-embedded examinations: judgemental and statistical approaches'. In H. Goldstein and T. Lewis (eds), *Assessment Problems, Developments, and Statistical Issues: A Volume of Expert Contributions*. Chichester: Wiley.

Cresswell, M. J. (2001). *Standard setting: Methods and issues*. Second Conference for the Association for Educational Assessment Europe. Krakow, Poland.

Crisp, G. (2007). *The E-assessment Handbook*. London: Continuum.

Cronbach, L. J. (1976). 'Measured mental abilities: lingering questions and loose ends'. In B. D. Davis and P. Flaherty (eds), *Human Diversity, its Causes and Social Significance: The Proceedings of a Series of Seminars*. Cambridge: Ballinger.

Crooks, T. (2011). 'Assessment for learning in the accountability era: New Zealand'. *Studies in Educational Evaluation*, 37 (1), 71–7.

Crooks, T., Kane, M. and Cohen, A. (1996). 'Threats to the valid use of assessments'. *Assessment in Education: Principles, Policies & Practice*, 3 (3), 265–85.

Daugherty, R. (2010). 'Summative assessment by teachers'. In P. Peterson, E. Baker and B. McGaw (eds), *International Encyclopedia of Education. Vol. 3*. (pp. 384–91). Oxford: Elsevier Science.

Deming, W. E. (1994). *The New Economics for Industry, Government, Education*. Cambridge, MA: Massachusetts Institute of Technology, Center for Advanced Engineering Study.

Department for Children, Schools and Families (DCSF) (2008). *The Assessment for Learning Strategy*. Available at: https://www.education.gov.uk/publications/eOrderingDownload/DCSF-00341-2008.pdf

Department for Children, Schools and Families (DCSF) (2009). *The Independent Review of the Primary Curriculum*, Available at: https://www.education.gov.uk/publications/standard/AbouttheDepartment/Page3/DCSF-00499-2009

Department for Education DfE (2011a). *Functional Skills*. Available at: http://www.education.gov.uk/16to19/qualificationsandlearning/functionalskills/a0064058/functional-skills.

Department for Education DfE (2011b). *GCSE and Equivalent Attainment by Pupil Characteristics in England 20010/11*. Available at: http://www.education.gov.uk/rsgateway/DB/SFR/s001057/index.shtml

Department for Education DfE (2012). *Year 1 phonics screening test*. Available at: http://media.education.gov.uk/assets/files/year%201%20phonics%20sample%20materials.pdf

Department for Education and Employment DfEE (2001). *Skills for Life: The National Strategy for Improving Adult Literacy and Numeracy Skills*. London: Department for Education and Employment.

Department for Innovation, Universities and Skills DIUS (2009). *Skills for Life: Changing Lives*. London: Department for Innovation, Universities and Skills.

Department of Education and Science (DES) (1987). *National Curriculum: Task Group on Assessment and Testing. A Report*. London: DES.

Department of Higher Education and Training South Africa (DHETSA) (2012). *National Certificates (Vocational), Assessment Guidelines*. Available at: http://www.dhet.gov.za/LinkClick.aspx?fileticket=vvnZP4fwAng%3D&tabid=451

Dewey, J. (1938). *Experience and Education*. New York: MacMillan.

Dewey, J., Boydston, J. A., Levine, B. and Steven M. C. (1988). *The Later Works of John Dewey 1925–1953: 1938–1939. Experience and Education, Freedom and Culture, Theory of Valuation, and Essays. Volume 13*. Carbondale, IL: Southern Illinois University Press.

Dewey, J., Boydston, J. A., Simon, H. F. and Kaplan, A. (1987). *The Later Works of John Dewey 1925–1953: 1934. Art as Experience. Volume 10*. Carbondale, IL: Southern Illinois University Press.

Dillon, H. (2007). *Life in the UK Test Practice Questions: Questions and Answers for British Citizenship and Settlement Tests*. London: Red Squirrel Publishing.

Ecclestone, K. (2010). *Transforming Formative Assessment in Lifelong Learning*. Maidenhead: McGraw-Hill.

Education Reform Act (1988). Available at: http://www.legislation.gov.uk/ukpga/1988/40/contents

Eraut, M. (2004). Transfer of Knowledge Between Education and Workplace Settings. In H. Rainbird, A. Fuller, and A. Munro (eds) *Workplace Learning in Context*. Abingdon: Routledge, pp. 201–21.

Ethos (2008). 'Final word: How do you solve a problem like … lack of basic skills?'. *Ethos Journal*. Available at: http://www.ethosjournal.com/archive/item/101-how-do-you-solve-a-problem-like-lack-of-basic-skills

European Union (2008). *European Qualifications Framework (EQF): Adopted by the European Parliament and Council on 23 April 2008*. Available at: http://ec.europa.eu/education/lifelong-learning-policy/doc44_en.htm

Flynn, J. R. (1999). 'Searching for justice: The discovery of IQ gains over time'. *American Psychologist*, 54 (1), 5–20.

Fuller, A. and Unwin, L. (1998). 'Reconceptualising apprenticeship: exploring the relationship between work and learning'. *Journal of Vocational Education & Training*, 50 (2), 153–73.

Futurelab (2007). *E-assessment – an update on research, policy and practice. Report 10*. Available at: http://archive.futurelab.org.uk/resources/documents/lit_reviews/Assessment_Review_update.pdf

Gardner, F. and Coombs, S. J. (2009). *Researching, Reflecting and Writing About Work: Guidance on Training Course Assignments and Research for Psychotherapists and Counsellors*. Hove: Routledge.

Gardner, H. (1983). *Frames of Mind: The Theory of Multiple Intelligences*. New York: Basic Books

Gardner, J., Harlen, W., Hayward, L., Stobart, G. and Montgomery, M. (eds) (2010). *Developing Teacher Assessment*. Maidenhead: Open University Press.

Gershon, R. C. (2005). 'Computer adaptive testing'. *Journal of Applied Measurement,* 6 (1), 109–27.

Gibbs, G. and Simpson, C. (2004). 'Conditions under which assessment supports students' learning'. *Learning and Teaching in Higher Education,* 1 (1), 3–31.

Gipps, C. (2012). *Beyond Testing: Towards a Theory of Educational Assessment, Classic Edition.* Abingdon: Routledge.

Gipps, C. and Murphy, P. (1994). *A Fair Test? Assessment, Achievement and Equity.* Buckingham: Open University Press.

Gipps, C. and Stobart, G. (2009). 'Families in assessment'. In C. Wyatt-Smith and J. Cumming (eds), *Educational Assessment in the 21st Century* (pp.105–18). London: Springer.

Gonczi, A. (2004). 'The new professional and vocational education'. In G. Foley (ed.), *Dimensions of Adult Learning: Adult Education and Training in a Global Era.* Maidenhead: Open University Press.

Goodhart, C. A. E. (1975). 'Problems of monetary management: the UK experience'. In *Papers in Monetary Economics. Volume I.* Reserve Bank of Australia.

Gould, S. J. (1996). *The Mismeasure of Man: Revised and expanded* (2nd edn). New York: Norton & Co.

Gravells, A. (2010). *Delivering Employability Skills in the Lifelong Learning Sector.* Exeter : Learning Matters.

Grek, S. (2009). 'Governing by numbers: the PISA "effect" in Europe'. *Journal of Education Policy,* 24 (1), 23–37.

Gronlund, N. E. and Waugh, C. K. (2009). *Assessment of Student Achievement* (9th edn). Upper Saddle River, NJ: Pearson.

Guskey, T. R. (2011). 'Five obstacles to grading reform'. *Educational Leadership,* 69 (3), 16–21.

Haahr, J. H., Nielsen, T. K., Jakobsen, S. T. and Hansen, M. E. (2005). *Explaining Student Performance: Evidence from the International PISA, TIMSS and PIRLS Surveys:* European Commission, Directorate General for Education and Culture. Available at: http://ec.europa.eu/education/pdf/doc282_en.pdf

Hanson, F. A. (1994). *Testing Testing: Social Consequences of the Examined Life.* Berkeley, CA: University of California Press.

Hargreaves, E. (2011). 'Teachers' classroom feedback: still trying to get it right'. *Pedagogies: An International Journal,* 7 (1), 1–15.

Harlen, W. (2006). 'On the relationship between assessment for formative and summative purposes'. In J. Gardner (ed.), *Assessment and Learning,* 103–17. London: Sage.

Hattie, J. and Timperley, H. (2007). 'The power of feedback'. *Review of Educational Research,* 77 (1), 81–112.

He, Q., Hayes, M. and Wiliam, D. (2011). *Classification accuracy in results from Key Stage 2 National Curriculum testing.* Available at: http://www.ofqual.gov.uk/downloads/category/193-reliability-compendium?download=1263%3Aclassification-accuracy-in-results-from-key-stage-2-national-curriculum-tests-march-2011

Heritage, M. (2010). *Formative Assessment: Making it Happen in the Classroom.* London: Corwin.

Herman, J. L. and Baker, E. L. (2009). 'Assessment policy: making sense of the Babel'. In G. Sykes, B. L. Schneider, D. N. Plank and T. G. Ford (eds), *Handbook of Education Policy Research*. London: Routledge.

Hodgson, A. and Spours, K. (2007). 'Specialised diplomas: transforming the 14–19 landscape in England?' *Journal of Education Policy*, 22 (6), 657–73.

House of Commons (2009). *National Curriculum: Fourth Report of Session 2008–09*. London: Stationery Office.

House of Commons Children, Schools and Families Committee. (CSFC) (2008). *Testing and Assessment: Third Report of Session 2007–2008*. London: Stationery Office.

Hutchinson, C. and Young, M. (2011). 'Assessment for learning in the accountability era: empirical evidence from Scotland'. *Studies in Educational Evaluation*, 37 (1), 62–70.

Isaacs, T. (2010). 'Educational assessment in England'. *Assessment in Education: Principles, Policy & Practice*, 17 (3), 315–34.

Izard, J. (2005). *Overview of test construction*. Available at: http://www.unesco.org/iiep/PDF/TR_Mods/Qu_Mod6.pdf

James, M., Black, P., Carmichael, P., Drummond, M.J., Fox, A., MacBeath, J., McCormick, R., Pedder, D., Procter, R., Swaffield, S., Swann, J. and Wiliam, D. (2007). *Improving Learning How to Learn: Classrooms, Schools and Networks*. London: Routledge.

JISC (2007). *Effective practice with e-assessment: An overview of technologies, policies and practice in further and higher education*. Available at: http://www.jisc.ac.uk/publications/programmerelated/2007/pub_eassesspracticeguide.aspx

Kane, M. (2001). 'Current concerns in validity theory'. *Journal of Educational Measurement*, 38 (4), 319–42.

Kluger, A. N. and DeNisi, A. (1996). 'The effects of feedback interventions on performance: a historical review, a meta-analysis, and a preliminary feedback intervention theory'. *Psychological Bulletin*, 119 (2), 254–84.

Kolb, D. A. (1984). *Experiential Learning: experience as the Source of Learning and Development*. Upper Saddle River, NJ: Prentice-Hall.

Konrad, J. (2000). 'Assessment and verification of national vocational qualifications: policy and practice'. *Journal of Vocational Education & Training*, 52 (2), 225–43.

Koretz, D. (2008). *Measuring Up: What Educational Testing Really Tells Us*. Cambridge, MA: Harvard University Press.

Koretz, D., McCaffrey, D. and Hamilton, L. (2001). *Toward a Framework for Validating Gains Under High-Stakes Conditions*. CSE Technical Report 551. Los Angeles, CA: Center for the Study of Evaluation, University of California.

Koretz, D., Stecher, B., Klein, S. and McCaffrey, D. (1994). 'The Vermont Portfolio Assessment Program: findings and implications'. *Educational Measurement: Issues and Practice*, 13 (3), 5–16.

Krathwohl, D. R., Bloom, B. S. and Masia, B. B. (1964). *Taxonomy of educational Objectives: The Classification of Educational Goals. Handbook II: The Affective Domain*. New York: Longman, Green.

Lamprianou, I. (2009). 'Comparability of examination standards between subjects: an international perspective'. *Oxford Review of Education*, 35 (2), 205–26.

Laurillard, D. (1993). *Rethinking University Teaching: A Framework for the Effective Use of Educational Technology.* London: Routledge.

Le Métais, J. (2002). *International Development in Upper Secondary Education: Context, Provision and Issues.* London: National Foundation for Educational Research.

Leighton, J. P. and Gierl, M. J. (2007). *Cognitive Diagnostic Assessment for Education: Theory and Applications.* Cambridge: Cambridge University Press.

Linn, R. L. (2000). 'Assessments and accountability'. *Educational Researcher,* 29 (2), 4–16.

Linn, R. L. (2001). 'A century of standardized testing: controversies and pendulum swings'. *Educational Assessment,* 7 (1), 29–38.

Linn, R. L., Baker, E. L. and Betebenner, D. W. (2002). *Accountability Systems: The Implications of Requirements of the No Child Left Behind Act of 2001.* Los Angeles, CA: CSE Technical Report 567. CRESST.

Linn, R. L., Baker, E. L. and Dunbar, S. B. (1991). 'Complex, performance-based assessment: expectations and validation criteria'. *Educational Researcher,* 20 (8), 15–21.

Lipnevich, A. A. and Smith, J. K. (2009). 'Effects of differential feedback on students' examination performance'. *Journal of Experimental Psychology: Applied,* 15 (4), 319–33.

Machin, S. and Vignoles, A. (2006). *Education Policy in the UK.* London: Centre for Economics of Education, London School of Economics.

Mansell, W. (2007). *Education by Numbers: The Tyranny of Testing.* London: Politico's Publishing.

Mansell, W. and James, M. with the Assessment Reform Group (2009). *Assessment in Schools. Fit for Purpose? A Commentary by the Teaching and Learning Research Programme.* London: Economic and Social Research Council, Teaching and Learning Research Programme.

Mayer, R. E. and Moreno, R. (2002). 'Aids to computer-based multimedia learning'. *Learning and Instruction,* 12 (1), 107–19.

McCabe, D. L. and Trevino, L. K. (1996). 'What we know about cheating in College'. *Change,* 28 (1), 28–33.

Messick, S. (1989). 'Validity'. In R. L. Linn (ed.), *Educational Measurement* (3rd edn). New York: MacMillan.

Miller, D., Linn, R. L. and Gronlund, N. E. (2009). *Measurement and Assessment in Teaching.* (10th edn) Upper Saddle River, NJ: Pearson Education.

Miller, G. E. (1990). 'The assessment of clinical skills/competence/performance'. *Academic Medicine,* 65 (9), 63–7.

Moss, P., Girard, B. and Haniford, L. (2006). 'Validity in educational assessment'. *Review of Research in Education,* 30, 109–62.

Mullis, I. V. S., Martin, M. O., Kennedy, A. M., Trong, K. L. and Sainsbury, M. (2009). *TIMSS 2011 Assessment Framework.* Chestnut Hill, MA: Boston College.

Munns, G. and Woodward, H. (2006). 'Student engagement and student self-assessment: the REAL framework'. *Assessment in Education: Principles, Policy & Practice,* 13 (2), 193–213.

National Foundation for Educational Research (NFER) (n.d.). *Assessment development: types of assessment. Attainment testing.* Available at: http://www.nfer.ac.uk/nfer/research/assessment/assessment-development/attainment-testing.cfm

key concepts in educational assessment

National Union of Teachers (2002). *The case against testing in England.* Available at: http://www.teachers.org.uk/resources/pdf/case_against_testing.pdf

Newton, P. E. (2007a). 'Clarifying the purposes of educational assessment'. *Assessment in Education: Principles, Policy & Practice,* 14 (2), 149–70.

Newton, P. E. (2007b). 'Contextualising the comparability of examination standards'. In P. Newton, J. A. Baird, H. Goldstein, H. Patrick and P. Tymms (eds), *Techniques for Monitoring the Comparability of Examination Standards.* London: QCA.

Newton, P. E. (2009). 'The reliability of results from National Curriculum testing in England'. *Educational Research,* 51 (2), 181–212.

Newton, P. E. (2010). 'Contrasting conceptions of comparability'. *Research Papers in Education,* 25 (3), 285–92.

Newton, P., Baird, J.-A., Goldstein, H., Patrick, H. and Tymms, P. (eds). (2007). *Techniques for Monitoring the Comparability of Examination Standards.* London: QCA.

Nicol, D. (2007a). 'E-assessment by design: using multiple-choice tests to good effect'. *Journal of Further and Higher Education,* 31 (1), 53–64.

Nicol, D. (2007b). 'Laying a foundation for lifelong learning: case studies of e-assessment in large 1st-year classes'. *British Journal of Educational Technology,* 38 (4), 668–78.

Nisbet, I. and Greig, A. (2007a). 'Educational qualification regulation'. In P. Vass (ed.), *Regulatory Review 2006/2007. 10th Anniversary Edition.* Bath: Centre for the Study of Regulated Industries, University of Bath.

Nisbet, I. and Greig, A. (2007b). *Regulation, Risk and Reputation, 2nd Annual Cambridge Conference on Regulation, Inspection and Improvement.* Peterhouse College, University of Cambridge.

Norcini, J. J. (2003). 'Work based assessment'. *British Medical Journal,* 326 (7392), 753–85.

Nuffield Review (2007). *Issues Paper 1: The New 14–19 Diplomas.* Available at: www.nuffieldfoundation.org/sites/default/files/files/1%20The%20New%2014-19%20Diplomas.pdf

Oates, T. (2011). 'Could do better: using international comparisons to refine the National Curriculum in England'. *Curriculum Journal,* 22 (2), 121–50.

OCNEMR (2011). *Internal verification.* Available at: http://www.ocnemr.org.uk/uFiles/file/Centre%20Handbook/CR%20Quality%20Assurance%20systems.pdf

OECD (2005). *Formative assessment: improving learning in secondary classrooms.* Available at: http://www.oecd.org/dataoecd/19/31/35661078.pdf

OECD (2011). *Programme for International Student Assessment (PISA).* Available at: www.pisa.oecd.org

Ofqual (2009). *National curriculum assessment: regulatory framework.* Available at: http://www.ofqual.gov.uk/files/2009-02-nc-assessments-rf.pdf

Ofqual (2010a). *Introducing Ofqual 2010/11.* Available at: http://www.ofqual.gov.uk/files/2010-07-22-introducing-ofqual.pdf

Ofqual (2010b). *Modified question papers: the future of language accessibility in the UK.* Available at: http://www.ofqual.gov.uk/downloads/category/42-comparability?downlo ad=835%3Amodified-question-papers-the-future-of-language-accessibility-in-the-uk

Ofqual (2010c). *National Curriculum assessment: code of practice.* Available at: http://www.ofqual.gov.uk/downloads/category/153-national-curriculum-?download= 465%3Anational-curriculum-assessments-code-of-practice-2010

Ofqual (2011). *GCSE, GCE, Principal Learning and Project Code of Practice.* Coventry: Ofqual. Available at: http://www.ofqual.gov.uk/downloads/category/93-codes-of-practice?download=680%3Agcse-gce-principal-learning-and-project-code-of-practice-2011

Ofqual (2012a). *A level reform consultation.* Available at: http://comment.ofqual.gov.uk/a-level-reform/

Ofqual (2012b). *Register of regulated qualifications.* Available at: http://register.ofqual.gov.uk/

Ofsted (2011). *The impact of the 'Assessing pupils' progress'* initiative. Available at: http://www.ofsted.gov.uk/resources/impact-of-assessing-pupils-progress-initiative

Ogg, T., Zimdars, A. and Heath, A. (2009). 'Schooling effects on degree performance: a comparison of the predictive validity of aptitude testing and secondary school grades at Oxford University'. *British Educational Research Journal,* 35 (5), 781–807.

Palm, T. (2008). 'Performance assessment and authentic assessment: a conceptual analysis of the literature'. *Practical Assessment, Research & Evaluation,* 13 (4), 1–11.

Papen, U. (2005). 'A critical reading of the Skills for Life strategy'. In U. Papen (ed.), *Adult Literacy as Social Practice: More Than Skills.* London: Routledge.

Perry, D. (2011). 'The basics of vocational assessment: a tool for finding the right match between people with disabilities and occupations'. Available at: http://www.ilo.org/public/english/region/asro/bangkok/ability/download/voc_assessment.pdf

PIRLS (2011). *Progress in International Reading Literacy Study 2011.* Available at: http://www.iea.nl/pirls_2011.html

Pryor, J. and Crossouard, B. (2008). 'A socio-cultural theorisation of formative assessment'. *Oxford Review of Education,* 34 (1), 1–20.

Qualifications and Curriculum Authority (QCA) (2004). *The statutory regulation of external qualifications in England, Wales and Northern Ireland.* Available at: www.qca.org.uk/libraryAssets/media/6944_regulatory_criteria_04(1).pdf

Qualifications and Curriculum Authority (QCA) (2006a). *Fairness by Design.* London: QCA.

Qualifications and Curriculum Authority (QCA) (2006b). *NVQ Code of Practice.* London: QCA.

Race, P., Brown, S. and Smith, B. (2005). *500 Tips on Assessment.* (2nd edn). London: RoutledgeFalmer.

Reynolds, C. R., Livingston, R. B. and Willson, V. L. (2005). *Measurement and Assessment in Education.* Boston, MA: Pearson/Allyn & Bacon.

Richardson, C. (ed.) (2003). *Whither Assessment?* London: QCA.

Ripley, M. (2006). *The four changing faces of e-assessment 2006–2016.* Available at: http://www.xplora.org/ww/en/pub/insight/thematic_dossiers/articles/e_assessment/eassessment2.htm

Roblyer, M. D., Edwards, J. and Havriluk, M.A. (2000). *Integrating Educational Technology into Teaching* (2nd edn). New Jersey: Merrill.

Rutkowski, L. and Rutkowski, D. (2010). 'Getting it "better": the importance of improving background questionnaires in international large-scale assessment'. *Journal of Curriculum Studies,* 42 (3), 411–30.

key concepts in educational assessment

Sadler, D. R. (1989). 'Formative assessment and the design of instructional systems'. *Instructional Science*, 18, 119–44.

Sadler, D. R. (1995). *Comparability of assessments, grades and qualifications*, AARE conference, Hobart, Tasmania.

Sadler, D. R. (2005). 'Interpretations of criteria-based assessment and grading in higher education'. *Assessment & Evaluation in Higher Education*, 30 (2), 175–94.

Sadler, D. R. (2009). 'Indeterminacy in the use of preset criteria for assessment and grading'. *Assessment & Evaluation in Higher Education*, 34 (2), 159–79.

Schön, D. A. (1983). *The Reflective Practitioner: How Professionals Think in Action*. New York: Basic Books.

Scoppio, G. (2002). 'Common trends of standardisation, accountability, devolution and choice in the educational policies of England, UK, California, USA, and Ontario, Canada'. *Current Issues in Comparative Education*, 2 (2), 254–66.

Scott, D. (2011). 'Assessment Reform: High-Stakes Testing and Knowing the Contents of Other Minds'. *Assessment Reform in Education, Education in the Asia-Pacific Region: Issues, Concerns and Prospects*, 14 (2), 155–63.

Sebba, J., Crick, R. D., Yu, G., Lawson, H., Harlen, W. and Durant, K. (2008). *Systematic review of research evidence of the impact on students in secondary schools of self and peer assessment. Technical report*. London: EPPI-Centre, Social Science Research Unit, Institute of Education, University of London.

Shavelson, R.J. (2008). Guest editor's introduction. *Applied Measurement in Education*, 21(4), 293–94.

SHEEO. (2003). *Issues, Priorities and Trends in State Higher Education*. Denver, CO: State Higher Education Executive Officers.

Smeyers, P. and Depaepe, M. (eds) (2008). *Educational research: the educationalization of social problems*. New York: Springer.

Smith, C. (1998). *Economics Without Frontiers*. Geneva: IB World.

Smith, E. and Gorard, S. (2005). '"They don't give us our marks": the role of formative feedback in student progress'. *Assessment in Education: Principles, Policy & Practice*, 12 (1), 21–38.

South African Qualifications Authority (SAQA). (2007). *Enhancing the efficacy and efficiency of the National Qualifications Framework: Joint Policy Statement by the Ministers of Education and Labour*. Available at: http://www.saqa.org.za/docs/policy/polstatement.pdf

Stobart, G. (2005). 'Fairness in multicultural assessment systems'. *Assessment in Education: Principles, Policy & Practice*, 12(3), 275–87.

Stobart, G. (2008). *Testing Times: The Uses and Abuses of Assessment*. Abingdon: Routledge.

Stobart, G. (2009). 'What is quality Assessment for Learning? The spirit vs the letter'. *Proceedings of the Chartered Institute of Educational Assessors*, London. Available at: http://www.ciea.co.uk

Stobart, G. (2011). *Feedback in Assessment for Learning (Presentation made in Oslo, Norway)*. Available at: http://www.udir.no/PageFiles/Vurdering%20for%20laring/Dokumenter/Nasjonal%20satsing/Gordon%20Stobart/2/Feedback%20Oslo%2009022011.pdf

Stobart, G., Elwood, J. and Quinlan, M. (1992). 'Gender bias in examinations: how equal are the opportunities?'. *British Educational Research Journal*, 18 (3), 261–76.

Strand, S. (2010). 'The limits of social class in explaining ethnic gaps in educational attainment'. *British Educational Research Journal*, 37 (2), 197–229.

Stray, C. (2001). 'The shift from oral to written examination: Cambridge and Oxford 1700–1900'. *Assessment in Education: Principles, Policy & Practice*, 8 (1), 33–50.

Swaffield, S. (2009). The misrepresentation of Assessment for Learning – and the woeful waste of a wonderful opportunity, *AIAA National Conference*. Bournemouth, UK.

Tan, K. H. K. (2004). 'Does student self-assessment empower or discipline students?'. *Assessment & Evaluation in Higher Education*, 29 (6), 651–62.

Taras, M. (2005). 'Assessment – summative and formative – some theoretical reflections'. *British Journal of Educational Studies*, 53 (4), 466–78.

Tattersall, K. (2007). 'A brief history of policies, practices and issues relating to comparability'. In P. Newton, J. A. Baird, H. Goldstein, H. Patrick and P. Tymms (eds), *Techniques for Monitoring the Comparability of Examination Standards* (pp. 42–96). London: QCA.

TIMSS (2011). *Trends in International Mathematics and Science Study 2011*. Available at: http://www.iea.nl/timss_2011.html

Torrance, H. (2007). 'Assessment as learning? How the use of explicit learning objectives, assessment criteria and feedback in post-secondary education and training can come to dominate learning'. *Assessment in Education: Principles, Policy & Practice*, 14 (3), 281–94.

Torrance, H. and Pryor, J. (1998). *Investigating Formative Assessment: Teaching, Learning and Assessment in the Classroom*. Buckingham: Open University Press.

Tummons, J. (2011). *Assessing Learning in the Lifelong Learning Sector* (3rd edn). Exeter: Learning Matters.

Van Gennip, N. A. E., Segers, M. S. R. and Tillema, H. H. (2009). 'Peer assessment for learning from a social perspective: the influence of interpersonal variables and structural features'. *Educational Research Review*, 4 (1), 41–54.

von Cranach, M. and Harré, R. (eds). (1982). *The Analysis of Action: European Studies in Social Psychology*. Cambridge: Cambridge University Press.

Wiliam, D. (1993). 'Validity, dependability and reliability in National Curriculum assessment'. *The Curriculum Journal*, 4 (3), 335–50.

Wiliam, D. (1996). 'Meanings and consequences in standard setting'. *Assessment in Education: Principles, Policy & Practice*, 3 (3), 287–308.

Wiliam, D. (2001). 'Reliability, validity, and all that jazz'. *Education 3–13*, 29 (3), 17–21.

Wiliam, D. (2008). 'Six degrees of integration: an agenda for joined up assessment'. In *Documents of Proceedings, Chartered Institute of Educational Assessors* (CIEA), conference, London. Available at: http://www.ciea.co.uk

Wiliam, D. (2009). *Assessment for Learning: Why, What and How?* London: Institute of Education.

Wiliam, D. (2010a). 'Standardized Testing and School Accountability'. *Educational Psychologist*, 45 (2), 107–22.

key concepts in educational assessment

Wiliam, D. (2010b). 'What Counts as Evidence of Educational Achievement? The Role of Constructs in the Pursuit of Equity in Assessment'. *Review of Research in Education*, 34 (1), 254–84.

Wiliam, D. (2011). 'What is assessment for learning?'. *Studies in Educational Evaluation*, 37 (1), 3–14

Wolf, A. (1995). *Competence-Based Assessment*. Buckingham: Open University Press.

Wolf, A. (2001). *Competence-based assessment*. Available at: http://www.heacademy. ac.uk/assets/documents/resources/heca/heca_cl25.pdf

Wolf, A. (2009). The role of the state in educational assessment, 19 October 2009. Cambridge Assessment Conference. Robinson College,Cambridge, UK.

Wolf, A. (2011). *Review of Vocational Education – The Wolf Report*. London: Department for Education.

Wood, P. (1991). 'The cooperating teacher's role in nurturing reflective teaching'. In B.R. Tabachnick and K. Zeichner (eds) *Issues and practices in inquiry-oriented teacher education*. London: Falmer Press, 202–10.

Wood, R. (1991). *Assessment and Testing: A Survey of Research*. Cambridge: Cambridge University Press.

Wright, R. J. (2007). *Educational Assessment: Tests and Measurements in the Age of Accountability*. New York: Sage.